Little Busybodies

by Jeanette Augustus Marks

CONTENTS

CHAPTER

NOTE.--We do not think it practicable to give classifications except as they exist unnamed in the above titles: (1) straight winged: locusts, grasshoppers, crickets, katydids; (2) tooth-shaped: dragon-flies; (3) ephemerals: may-flies; (4) half-winged: leaf and tree hoppers; (5) nerve-winged: lace-wings, ant-lions, and caddis-worms; (6) two-winged: flies and mosquitoes; (7) scaly winged: butterflies and moths; (8) sheath-winged: beetles; (9) membranous-winged: bees, wasps, and ants.

A WORD TO THE CHILDREN AND THE WISE

We hope that the children who read this book will like the boys and girls who are in it. They are real, and the good times they have are real, as any boy or girl who has lived out-of-doors will know. And the stories are true. Peter is not always good. But do you expect a child always to be good? We do not. Sometimes, too, the frolics turn in to a scramble to catch a dragon-fly that will not be caught, and there are accidents. Also, Betty and Jack work hard to win a prize which the guide gives to the child who learns most about ants.

Of course it would be impossible for five children to go in search of locusts, grasshoppers, crickets, katydids, dragon-flies, May-flies, leaf-hoppers, lace-wings, caddis-worms, butterflies, beetles, bees, wasps--and so many other six-legged creatures that among them they have wings and legs enough to fill a new Pandora's box--without having a good deal happen. And a good deal does happen. It is all true enough, and every word about the six-legged busybodies is true as true. The other books, too, that come after this in our Story-Told Science Series will be every word true.

And we who wrote this book? Well, we, too, have been children. We used to climb trees and turn somersaults; why--But that is another story! And we remember so well what it used to be like to have to learn dull things we did not wish to know. So we said to ourselves, as we looked over our spectacles at each other, "No, they sha'n't be told a single uninteresting fact; they sha'n't be dull, poor dears, as we were so long ago, before we put on spectacles and began to call ourselves wise."

And so, although we sat down and wrote a book just about long enough for a school-year's work; although we felt very proud because our stories had more wonderful six-legged creatures than any book written for children; although we took pains to have in the book only such little creatures as any one of us could see any day; although we hoped that mothers and teachers would say, "At last, this is a book the children and I can like and find useful!" or, "There, that will help as a starting-point to tell about the bees and the flowers!" or, "This story about the flies will teach the children what it means to be clean!" Although, I say, we hoped all these things, yet our chief hope was that we might give all sorts of children a good time.

So we put our spectacles on and looked very wise, and took a quantity of ink on our pens and began to write. And we wrote and wrote and wrote. And part of the time, while one of us was writing and hoping the stories would be so interesting the children would want to write about them, too, the other was drawing and labelling each sketch so plainly that any child could understand it, even if the ears were quite where they could not be expected to be, or there were more eyes than, seemingly, one creature ought to have, or wings and legs served to make music, as no sensible child could possibly guess.

And now we can't do better than wish you a good time before we say good-bye. We wish you to enjoy all the frolics, to feel how jolly it is to be out-of-doors in the woods and fields and lakes, climbing, canoeing, picnicing, and swimming.

But still more, we hope that you will realize that more wonderful than the most wonderful fairy story ever told is the marvel of the created life of these little insects; we want you to come to know something of their joys and troubles; we want you to learn how to be kind to them, and how they may be useful to you; and we want you to find out for yourselves the places they take in the great plan of creation.

In other words, we want you to think and feel about the lives of these six-legged busybodies, and see for yourselves how much even a butterfly can add to the interest and beauty of living. Does this seem a little bit like a sermon? Well, you see, we forgot we had kept on our spectacles so long, and somehow spectacles always turn into sermons. Perhaps it is because both begin with the letter S.

And now this is all of our short word to the wise. We expect to make each one of our books better than the last, and you can help us to do this by writing any suggestions you may have. We shall be glad to hear from children, big or little.

J. M. and J. M.

South Hadley, Massachusetts, January 27, 1909.

LITTLE BUSYBODIES

I

THE JOURNEY

"It will be stories all summer, won't it?" said Betty to her mother.

"Yes, dear."

"And hunting, too?" said Jimmie.

"Hunting with your new gun and hunting with your camera."

Jimmie unfastened the case of his new camera and looked in. What a beautiful one it was, and what pictures he meant to take, and how the camera would impress Ben Gile! Jimmie looked about proudly. He knew no other boy in that whole great train had a camera like the one his father had given him.

"Mother, when will it be lunch?" asked Betty.

"Luncheon so soon!"

"I'm as hungry as a bear," declared Jimmie.

"And hear Kitty mewing; she's hungry, too." Betty looked at the big round basket, whose cover kept restlessly stirring.

"Did you leave something in the baggage-car for Max to eat?" Mrs. Reece asked Jimmie.

"Yes, mum. It's one o'clock; can't we have something now?"

"As late as that! No wonder you chickens are hungry for--"

"Chicken!" squealed Betty.

"And ham sandwiches!" added Jimmie.

"And chocolate cake!"

"And root-beer!"

"And peppermints!"

"Ssh!" said Mrs. Reece, "or every one in the car will know what little piggies you are. Ask Lizzie for the basket."

[Illustration: A. Outer wing of locust. B. Inner wing of locust. C. Sideview of locust. a. Antenna. b. Simple eye. c. Compound eye. d. Thorax. e. Abdomen. f. Breathing pore. g. Ear. D. Hind leg of locust.]

Every minute the air was growing cooler. The children could smell the pine woods, and once in a while the train flashed by a great big sawmill, or a lake set like a sapphire in the deep green of the forests. And the hills were rolling nearer and nearer in great shadows. The children ate their luncheon contentedly, looking out of the windows and thinking of the mountains there would be to climb, the ponds, the streams to fish, the pictures to take, and the stories they were to hear the summer long.

"Mother," said Betty, eating her second piece of chocolate cake--"mother, what will Ben Gile tell us this summer?"

"Let me see," said her mother, "perhaps it will be about the little creatures-- grasshoppers and katydids, butterflies and bees."

"Goody!"

"Pooh!" said Jimmie, "I don't see what you want to know of those old things. I'd much rather hear about porcupines. There isn't anything to say about a grasshopper except that it hops."

"Isn't there, my son? Well, that shows that you don't use your eyes. Suppose some one said there was nothing to say about you except that you whistle?"

"Well, what is there about an old grasshopper, anyhow?"

"I don't know, but Ben will."

"But tell us something, mum," urged Jimmie, who loved his mother dearly, and was certain she knew more than anybody else, in part because she had been to college, but chiefly because she was his mother.

"Let me see," said Mrs. Reece, "I shall have to think about it." Both of the children came as close to her as they could, while she continued:

"What a strange world it would be if there were no insects in it! We should have no little crickets chirping in the sunny fields or in the dark corners and cracks of our houses. There would be no katydids singing all night, no clacking of the locusts in the tall grass along dusty roads, no drowsy hum of bees. There would be no little ants and big ants digging out underground tunnels and carrying the grains of sand as far from their doorways as possible. There would be no brightly colored moths and butterflies flitting from flower to flower. We should find no sparkling fairy webs spun anew for us every morning."

"But, mother, all these creatures aren't insects," said Jimmie.

"Yes, they are, dear. It is hard to believe that they all belong to the same family called insecta, but they do."

"Mother, what's that word mean?"

"It doesn't mean anything more than cut up into parts. You see, Betty, all these insect bodies are made up of separate rings joined nicely together. If you look carefully you will find that behind the head there is another distinct part. This is called the thorax, which means chest. Behind that there is a pointed part of the body, which is called the abdomen. Then, if you look again, you will see that all these little creatures are alike in that they have six jointed legs."

"And are they all good, like the bee and the butterfly?" asked Betty, who wasn't always a good little girl herself, and who thought it would be much nicer if insects were naughty sometimes.

"Not all, dear," answered Mrs. Reece; "some do us real service, but others are troublesome; insects are such hungry little fellows, and they don't have chocolate cake every day to keep them from getting hungry. They are hungry when they are babies and hungry when they grow up. Some eat all they can see--like a little boy I know--and some prefer the tender leaves and twigs. Some care only for the sweet sap flowing into the new leaves and buds. And still others like best the tender new roots of plants."

"Mother, what are the baddest ones?" asked Betty.

"Pooh! I know," said Jimmie; "the beetles are, because they eat everything. Why, they'd eat the buttons off your coat or the nose off your face or--"

"Jim! Jim! do tell the truth! The beetles, and bugs, too, are the most troublesome. Many of the bugs are such tiny little creatures that it is hard to realize that they can hurt a plant. But bugs have sucking beaks. With these beaks they bore into the leaves or the buds of the plant, and then by means of tiny muscles at the back of the mouth they pump up the sap. To be sure, one little pump could do no harm; but think of millions of little sucking beaks, millions of little pumps busy at work on a single plant! Do you remember the pansies mother had in the winter, and how they were all covered by green plant-lice? Well, those are bugs called aphids. You remember they were pale green, just the color of the plant, and so transparent and soft they looked most harmless. The scale insects are very troublesome, too, but mother doesn't know anything about them."

"Oh, I know what they are," announced Jimmie, "they get into the fruit trees."

"And sometimes onto shrubs, too. Mother has heard of a scale insect out in California which has been a great nuisance to fruit-growers. A certain ladybug finds this cottony-cushion scale a tender morsel, so many ladybugs were taken out there to help the owners of the fruit farms get rid of the scale."

"Did they carry them all the way out, mother?"

"Yes," answered Jimmie; "they got a Pullman car for them, and Mr. and Mrs. Ladybug and family travelled in style."

"Mother, tell Jim to be still." Betty, not unlike other little sisters, hated to be teased by her brother.

"And now, let me see," said Mrs. Reece. "I don't know that I can tell you any more until I know more myself. Yes, I do know what baby beetles are called. They are called grubs, and they live in the ground until it is time for them to turn into grown-up beetles. While they are babies they eat as much and as fast as they can, as no baby but a beetle should. The more they eat the sooner they come out into the bright world as a June-bug or some other kind of beetle. They eat all the tender little roots they can find. This is very nice--"

"For Mary Ann, but rather hard on Abraham."

"You horrid boy," said Betty, "you don't even let me hear a story in peace! It's very nice what, mother?"

"It's very nice for the little grubs, but it's rather hard on the plants, for if too many roots are nibbled away the plants die. The caterpillars are great eaters, too."

Betty leaned over and whispered something to her mother; then they both giggled.

"I know what you're saying," said Jimmie, but after that he was quieter.

"Sometimes a caterpillar will thrive on just one kind of a plant; it may be carrot, it may be milkweed. On that it feeds until it has grown as large as possible. Then it spins itself a nice silken cocoon, or rolls itself up in a soft leaf and takes a long, long nap. And now it is time for us to take a nap, too, for we shall soon reach Bemis, and then there will be still two long lakes to cross and a carry to walk."

II

RANGELEY VILLAGE

The next morning great was the stir in the town, for it was known by the village children that Betty and Jimmie had come, and by the grown-ups that Mrs. Reece was there. All winter long the children had looked forward to their coming, for it meant jolly times: picnics, parties, expeditions, and games. Then, too, Ben Gile would begin to tell them wonderful things. Through the winter he had been teaching school, and it was only when the ice broke up in the big lake and the beavers decided to stop sleeping that Ben Gile came back to his guiding.

There was great excitement about Turtle Lodge. Lizzie kept flying out with rugs, and then forgetting they hadn't been brushed and flying in again. The cat was playing croquet with the balls and spools of an open work-basket, and Max had discovered an old straw hat which tasted very good to him. Only Mrs. Reece kept her head and stayed indoors, moving about quietly from room to room, putting the house in that beautiful order which little children never think about.

Out on the grass that sloped down to the street, which, in its turn, tumbled head over heels down to the lake, Betty and Jimmie were playing with their playmates. They were all so wild with joy that every time Jimmie saw another boy he shouted, "Come over!" when the boy was coming, anyway, just as fast as he could.

Up, up from the foot of the lake climbed an old man; up, up, up the steep street he came, his white hair shaking and shining in the brisk June breeze, his long, white beard caught every once in a while by the wind and tossed sideways.

"Mother," called Jimmie, "Ben Gile is coming!"

Out came Mrs. Reece to greet the old man.

Then, one by one, the children spoke with Ben Gile.

"You're having a good time before you can say Jack Robinson, aren't you?"

"Yes, sir," came in a chorus of voices. Then, "Tell us a story; tell us a story!"

"Not to-day," said the old man. "Why, you want a story before you've had time to turn around."

Betty stuck her head out from behind her mother. "Mother said you would tell us about crickets and moths, and everything."

"Well, well, well," murmured the old man, "did she? But I can't tell a story to-day. I'll tell you, though, something, so that when you come to collect the little creatures you'll know what to do. All sit down."

They all sat down cross-legged on the ground, the old man in the middle.

"Here, you big Jim-boy, catch me that butterfly."

There was a wild rush, and the bright wings were soon caught.

"There, you've torn off one of its legs," said the old man.

Jimmie looked troubled. "I didn't mean to, sir."

"Do you know how it hurts to have your leg torn off, boy? Do you know, children?"

"No," came in a chorus.

The guide took out a piece of paper and drew a picture on it. "There, every part of that little fellow's body I've drawn has muscles, such fine muscles no naked eye could ever see them. I'll show them to you under the microscope in my cabin. Those muscles move the body, and each muscle is controlled by threads, still more fine, called nerves."

The old man reached out like a flash and pinched Jimmie.

"Ouch!" cried the boy, and there was a shout of laughter from the children.

"You felt that?"

"I guess I did," said Jim, sulkily.

"Well, that's because you're made something the same way this butterfly is. When anything hurts us it's because some of our nerves are hurt, and quick as a flash the news travels to the brain, and we try to get away from the thing that causes pain--a pinch, perhaps, or, still worse, the hurt of a poor leg that has been torn off."

"But a butterfly hasn't any brain," objected Jimmie, who was still cross.

"Hasn't it? Well, we'll see. Now, you watch my pencil." He pointed to the head of the butterfly. "This little fellow has a very tiny brain there. Also running through the body, from end to end, is a little tube through which the food passes. It is in the head above this tube where the tiny brain is, and from which two little threads run down around the tube and join to form another little knot of nerve cells like that of the brain. Then, from this second one there runs a series of little knots united by fine threads the entire length of the body, one in each ring of the body. Do you understand that?"

"Yes," piped up Betty, "mother told us an insect is made up of rings, and-- and--" she stammered, surprised at her own boldness, "the word means cut up into parts."

"Good! Why, that's a real bright girl. Well, from each one of these knots nerves go to the muscles of the body."

"It's just like a lot of beads on a string," said Hope Stanton.

"So it is, child. So, you see, if we handle an insect roughly, squeezing it too hard, or breaking a leg or a wing, a message is sent to one of these little beads or knots or nerve cells, and the poor, helpless creature suffers pain."

"But I didn't mean to hurt that butterfly!"

"No, of course you didn't. The only way to do," said the old man, "is to catch them in a net. Make it of bobinet with a rounded bottom, sewing it to a wire ring and fastening it to a handle that is the right weight and length for your arm."

"But then, after you caught it, how could you keep it, sir?" asked Betty.

"There are two merciful ways," said the old man, "of killing insects, but neither way is safe for children to try. Put a few drops of chloroform on a piece of cotton under a tumbler turned upside down. Put the insect inside. It will soon fall asleep without pain. The other is a cyanide bottle. I have one down at the cabin. It must be kept tightly corked and never smelled. The cyanide in the bottle is hard and dry. Several insects may be put into the bottle at the same time. Once there they die very quickly. After large insects are killed the wings should be folded over the back, and they should be placed in a little case like this. See, I'm folding a piece of paper to form a three-cornered case. Then I bend down one edge to keep the little case closed."

At this moment out flew Lizzie with a curtain which she was going to shake.

"Here, here!" shouted the old man, "don't shake that; catch that caterpillar on it. I want it."

Lizzie made a good-natured grab at the caterpillar, and then there was a cry of pain. "Oh, begorra, begorra, I'm stung by a wasp, I am! Ow!" But she still kept tight hold of the caterpillar as she danced about.

"No," said the guide, "you're not stung by any wasp. Bring me that! There, open your hand. You see, the caterpillar stung you."

"Oh my, what a beauty!" exclaimed the children. "But caterpillars don't sting."

"Oh yes, they do," continued Ben Gile, with a twinkle in his eye; "ask Lizzie." Lizzie was looking at the palm of her hand, which showed how badly it had been stung.

"Now, you see, we'll need something to pick up these little creatures with--a pair of forceps or something of that kind. At least, you must be very careful."

"And what else do we need?" asked the children.

"A little hand lens will magnify the small parts of an insect a great deal. It will show you all the tiny hairs on the body, and the little rings and the feelers and the facets of the eyes, and many another wonderful thing."

"What are we going to put the bugs in?" inquired Jimmie.

"Lizzie will get you a small wooden box," said Mrs. Reece.

Lizzie went off grumbling something about guides and bites and insects, but soon she came back with a nice box, and in a minute all the children's heads were clustered about Ben Gile as he showed them how to line the box with a layer of cork, how to steam the insects a little if they were dry, and then how to put the long, slender pins through the chest of the insect and stick it into the cork.

III

THE LITTLE ARMY

Ben Gile shook his head. As his hair was long and white, and his hands moved with his head, just as if he were a lot of dried branches moving in the wind, it was enough to frighten little Betty. "Plagues of Egypt! Plagues of Egypt!" he kept muttering. Now, Betty had been to school a long time--I think it must have been as much as two whole years, which is a very long time for school and a very short time for climbing trees--now, Betty had been to school and knew better. She crept behind a big beech-tree, but she stuck her little head out and said, in a trembling voice:

"It was locusts, sir, wasn't it--and wild honey?"

Betty wasn't at all certain that any kind of honey could be a plague.

"It was locusts, child--yes, you're right," answered the old man. "Locusts it was; but you eat wild honey."

Betty came out from behind the tree and whispered, "You eat them both?"

"So men did in the Bible," said Ben Gile, and washing his sugar-pails, and putting his maple sugar camp--a very sweet place for a little girl to be when there are still piles of maple sugar packed away on the shelves--in order for the summer.

In all her short life Betty had never known another old man like him. In the winter he taught school; in spring he made maple sugar; in summer he was guiding about the ponds or looking up into the trees most of the time; and in the fall he cut wood before he went back to teaching; but what was oddest of all to Betty was that he knew the squirrels and deer and rabbits as well as he seemed to know little girls or little boys. There was a story told in those woods about his taming even a trout so that one morning it hopped out of the water and followed him everywhere he went--hop, hop, flop behind him. And in the evening, as Ben Gile and his tame trout were passing by the pond again, the trout fell in and was drowned. But, dear me, that is a fish story, and you mustn't believe any fish stories whatever except those your father tells! Still, if your grandpa is fond of fishing, you may believe his fish stories, too.

[Illustration: A. A locust. B. Cast-off skin of a young locust.]

Betty came out farther from behind the tree. "Please, sir, do you eat grasshoppers?"

"Not yet, my dear." The old man's eyes twinkled. "I knew a little boy once"-- Betty was wondering whether this old man had ever been a little boy himself--"I knew a little boy once who wasn't afraid to swallow even a caterpillar, but I think that little boy never thought of eating a grasshopper." The old man shook his head gravely. "No, not a grasshopper."

"Please, sir," said Betty, coming right up to the bucket he was washing in the brook--"please, sir, do you know any stories about grasshoppers?"

Ben Gile laid his finger along his nose and thought. Betty was sure he knew a hundred million stories, and that he could tell her something about anything she might ask for in all the world.

"Well, once upon a time," the old man began, "there was another old man who was a great deal wiser than I am, and a great deal richer, my dear, for he owned a whole kingdom and lived in a palace, and his name was--"

"Solomon!" called out Betty, dancing up and down, out of pride in her own wisdom.

"Right! And this other old man said:

"There are four things which are little upon the earth, but they are exceedingly wise:

"The ants are a people not strong, yet they prepare their meat in the summer;

"The conies are but a feeble folk, yet make they their houses in the rocks;

"The locusts have no king, yet go they forth all of them by bands;

"The spider taketh hold with her hands and is in kings' palaces."

"But that's not a story."

The guide shook his head. "You don't know a story, child, when you hear one. It began, 'Once upon a time,' didn't it?"

"Yes, sir; but please tell me another."

"Well, there are others in the Bible, my dear, about locusts and grasshoppers."

"But, please, sir," said Betty, who was almost ready to cry, she was so teased--"please tell me one of your own stories."

Ben Gile began to swash his bucket up and down, up and down, in the stream until the water fairly rocked. Then he pulled the bucket out of the water, set it beside him, and reached out after a locust.

"Here he is." There was a long pause. Betty thought he would never go on. "Well, once upon a time there was a little army and all its uniforms were brown and green, and from the meanest soldier in the ranks to the lieutenant-commander this little army was made up of insects who belonged to the same tribe. Let me see--there were the grasshoppers and the locusts and the katydids and the crickets."

"Please, sir, were they cousins?"

"I think they were, my dear. Yes, first cousins, and, unlike even my first cousins, they all have wings, and straight wings like this."

The guide gently spread out one of the wings.

"Just where the back of your chest is these wings grow--two pairs of wings, my dear, and two pairs of wings mean a good deal more than two pairs of new shoes. This first pair is straight and narrow and hard, because it is meant to cover the gauzy wings underneath. Puff!"

Away flew the locust.

"You see, he doesn't use his first pair, but holds them out straight from his body while he spreads out the gauzy ones like a--like a--"

"Fan!" shouted Betty, quite forgetting the tiny squirrel who had come up near her, and, at her shout, nearly jumped out of his little red jacket.

"A yellow fan," said the old man. "And some have a red fan. Well, I think," said he, reaching for his pail, "there isn't going to be any more of this story."

"Not any more? But there must be more, sir; I've seen hundreds and hundreds of them on a dusty road, and, please, they're just the color of the dirt."

The guide shook his head. "Not to-day."

By this time Betty was so eager to have him go on that she had forgotten all about being afraid of him. "And when they whir up from the road, sir, they say, 'Clack! clack! clack!'"

The old man made a sound like the noise of a locust.

"How does it make its mouth move, sir?"

"It doesn't make its mouth move, child. It makes the noise by striking the edges of the gauzy wings and hard wing covers together. See, this way!" And the old man struck his arm and leg together. "It has another fiddle, too, which it uses when it makes the long, rasping, drowsy sound of summer days. Then it rubs the rough edges of its hind leg against the edge of its wing-cover."

"Please, is it happy, then?" asked Betty.

"Just as happy as a healthy locust, who lives in long, sweet-smelling grass and is contented with his own singing, can be, and that is very happy."

"Oh!" said Betty, "it doesn't use its mouth, then? Jimmie said it did."

"Jimmie's a stupid boy. See this fellow." The old man held the locust toward Betty. "With its upper lip, broad, you see; and there is the lower lip made in two scallops, and there's a short feeler on either side, and another pair of soft jaws with a feeler. Hidden away under those parts is a pair of dark-brown, horny jaws which open like two big swinging gates."

"What makes them so big?"

"The better to eat you with, my dear." The guide worked his jaws until Betty, half afraid and half pleased, screamed and ran behind a tree. "Oh, how they can eat!" growled the old man, "more than any little girl or boy I ever knew! Years and years ago, when your mamma was a baby, they mounted up into the air from the Rocky Mountains and flew eastward in a great cloud. Down they swooped upon the fertile valleys in rustling hordes, and ate everything in sight--grass, grains, vegetables, and bushes. They ate and ate and ate until they had eaten up fifty million dollars' worth of food, and the poor farmer could hear nothing but the sound of the chewing of those ever-swinging jaws. Now, be off, little girl, or my pails won't be clean."

"Oh, please, sir, just tell me how they jump and breathe."

"Dear, dear, see this fellow!" He had wet a little grain of maple sugar, and a tiny meadow grasshopper which had alighted on his knee was pushing the sweet stuff into its mouth with both fore legs. "Child, you must never," said the old man, savagely, "push your food in that way."

"Please, sir," answered Betty, "I never do, because I eat with my fork and my knife. Please, sir, are they happy when they jump?"

"Looks like a horse, doesn't it?" asked the old man. "It's made for jumping. Think of all the training it takes to make a jumper of your brother at school. Well, this chap can jump ten times as far. It's born with a better jump than the longest-legged boy you ever saw. But the locust might get its head cut off when jumping if it weren't for this little saddle that covers the soft part of the neck. Mr. Locust can't always look before he leaps, as a little girl can, and the knife edge of a blade of grass would cut its head right off if it weren't for this saddle. See, here are its long leaping-legs, and on the back edge of these are some spines to keep it from slipping, and the feet are padded with several soft little cushions that keep it from chin-chopping itself to pieces when it lands after a long jump. And here, my dear, are little rest-legs just behind the front legs. With these Mr. Locust hangs on to a blade of grass when tired--a fine idea, child; every little boy and girl ought to have some rest-legs like the locust. And the locust has some extra eyes, too."

Ben Gile was going so fast now that Betty was listening to him, mouth open, as he pointed with a blade of grass to one thing after another.

"You see, the locust has two big eyes, and there in the middle of the forehead it has three little eyes, and with five eyes there isn't much it can't see. And here on the body are two tiny shining oval windows. These are ear-laps, and that, my dear, is the way it hears. And upon the sides of the body (the thorax--that is, just the chest) and his abdomen are tiny holes. The air enters through these, and that is the way Mr. Locust breathes."

"Oh," said Betty, "then it hasn't got any nose? I thought everything in the world had a nose."

"And this little body," the old man went on, "is as strong as a grub hoe. With it the locust makes holes in fence rails, logs, stumps, and the earth, and in those holes mother locust lays her eggs. See, those four spines are for boring holes. With these Mrs. Locust bores a hole in the ground, and then with these same spines she guides the bundles of eggs into the hole and covers them up with a gummy stuff. There the eggs stay until next spring, when, my dear, out comes a little hopper with no wings, and this little hopper is called a nymph. It grows and splits its skin, grows and splits its skin, and with its new skin--it has five or six skins, and leaves all its old clothes hanging around on the bushes--its wings grow bigger and bigger. At last it flies off just as its mother and father did a year ago."

Ben Gile tossed the locust into the air and called out, "Shoo!" clapping his hands loudly together. Out from the woods came two baby deer, a wise, gentle old cow; from the cabin came a mother cat and three kittens and a big black dog; and from the trees scampered down a half a dozen squirrels.

"Time for dinner."

Betty went up to him and whispered something in his ear. The old man nodded his head solemnly, and the little girl went trotting along the path to Rangeley Village.

IV

FIDDLERS

There was the greatest scurrying around in the fields on the edge of the woods about Ben Gile's cabin. Little girls and boys were flitting hither and thither with pretty nets and small boxes strapped over their shoulders. Inside the boxes there seemed to be just as much hopping about as there was outside.

By-and-by the guide put his head out of his cabin door and called, "How many have you?"

"Oh, lots and lots!" the children answered.

"Bring them in." And the children trooped into the cabin, which they thought quite the most wonderful place in the world. Its walls were lined with books and cases. The books were not only in English, but also in French, German, Italian, Latin, Greek, and other languages, and the cases were filled with scores of specimens, the most beautiful butterflies, moths, beetles, birds, flowers, and rare stones. The floor of the cabin was covered by different kinds of skins. Besides, there were telescopes, field-glasses, magnifying-glasses, specimen cases, old weapons, and a flute. And by the great wide fireplace, in front of which the guide was cooking biscuits and cookies in a reflector oven, lay several kittens, the old black dog, Thor, and a dappled fawn which Thor was licking.

"Those crickets sound like pop-guns," said the old man, slipping more cookies into the oven and setting a pan of biscuits on a shelf by the hearth.

"Oh, please," said little Hope, "we've got bushels of them!"

"Now we'll let those cookies bake while we 'tend to the fiddlers. Are four pans of cookies enough for five children?"

"Yes, yes."

"Now, Hope, let me have your bushel box. H'm," he murmured, peeping in, "all dressed for the party. What color?"

"Brown, sir."

"Black, too," said Betty; "and on a few," she added, "there's a stripe or a weeny spot of color."

"Oho!" exclaimed the old man, "what have we here?" He took a pale little creature from Hope's basket.

"Why, it's white and green tinted," called Jimmie. "That isn't a cricket."

"Isn't it? Well, it's a first cousin which lives in the trees and loves its tree home so much, like the sensible little fellow it is, that it sings 'Tr-e-e-e, tr-e-e-e,' as fast as it can trill all summer long. But it is very harmful to the tree, because when egg-laying time comes it cuts a long slit in the trees in which to lay its eggs. Just a minute!" The old man shifted the position of the baker, and out came such a good odor of cookies that all the children sniffed with delight. "Here, Jack," he said, to a brown little fellow in ragged clothes and bare feet, "you have a singer in your box."

"I didn't catch but one," said the lad.

"Briers aren't good for bare legs, are they? Never mind, your crickets won't eat one another."

"Eat one another?" cried the children.

"Yes, crickets are cannibals, like some other insects, and they frequently eat a near relation or a friend, as the people in the Fiji Islands used to do. This is a nice brown little chap, Jack. Do you know how he makes his music?"

"Why, I suppose," said the boy, "he opens his mouth the way Mr. Tucker does in the church choir, and--"

There was a shout of laughter from Jimmie, who was sure he knew a great deal.

"Well," said the guide to Jim, "then how does it make its music, since you know?"

"Not with its mouth."

"Then how?"

"I don't know, sir," stammered Jimmie, who found he didn't know as much as he thought he did.

"When Mr. Cricket sings," went on the hermit, "it lifts its two wing covers so that the edges meet like the pointed roof of a house. Then your little fiddler, Jack, rubs one edge against the other."

All this time Peter Beech had been waving his hand about, the way children do in school, and giving big sniffs.

"Please, sir, the cookies are burning."

"Bless my soul!" The guide whisked the cookies away.

"Please, sir," said Jack, "are we going to have something soon?" Jack did not look as if he had his share of food to eat, for he was as thin as the fawn which had curled up near him. Jack had twelve brothers and sisters, and a father who wasn't what he ought to be, so there were times when there was no food for Jack.

"Yes, my son," said the guide, kindly, for the old man could guess how hungry the lad was. "But, first, where do you suppose the crickets and katydids have their ears?"

"Near those big eyes," called Peter.

"No, no, on the joint of the fore leg is a little membrane, which is just a thinner, tighter place in the skin of the leg. There!" Ben Gile had the fore leg of Jack's cricket stretched under the magnifying-glass. The children could see plainly the film of tight skin. "Underneath the thin, tight skin is a fine nerve which, when the air makes the skin shake, changes the motion into sound. Mrs. Cricket listens with her fore leg while Mr. Cricket sings his love-song to her."

At this the children laughed and laughed, and comical little Peter put up his leg as if listening.

"Here, Pete, give me your box. Do you remember what I told you about Mrs. Locust, Betty, and the way she lays her eggs?"

"Yes, sir. She has four straight spines at the end of her body, and after she has bored a hole with her body she guides the eggs in with the four spines."

"Good! Well, Mrs. Cricket wears at the end of her body a long spear. See this cricket of Peter's. Now she bores her hole with this spear and then guides her eggs carefully into the hole. Why, see here, Pete, what have you got here?"

The children gazed eagerly over the old man's shoulder.

"My, isn't it like velvet!" exclaimed Peter.

"And isn't it brown!" added Hope.

"But look at its stumpy front legs!" called Jack, who had forgotten his empty stomach in the excitement about this little creature, which looked like a cricket and yet was so different.

"And its little beads of eyes!" said Betty.

"Do you know what it is?" No one knew. "Well, it's a mole cricket. You rarely ever see one because they live underground and bore their way along just like moles, leaving tiny tracks and nibbling the roots of tender plants. You see, it doesn't need eyes any more than the mole does. But it does need those thickened fore legs to do its underground digging. Now, children, run out into the fields and let your crickets go. Be careful not to hurt them. We'll have supper, and after supper we'll catch a katydid."

Out ran the children. Soon they were setting the long wooden tables under the trees with delicious trout the boys had caught, with hot biscuits and jugs of maple syrup, with berries and cookies, with milk from the old cow, who, contentedly chewing her cud, was looking at them through the low crotch of a tree, and with little cakes of maple sugar which the guide had moulded into the shape of hearts.

V

HOW KATY DID

Never did trout, cookies, and maple sugar disappear so quickly; never were such appetites; never such laughing, and such interesting stories told by the guide.

"Hush!" said Ben Gile. "Do you hear that?"

"Yes," cried Peter.

"What is it?"

"It's a katydid," said Betty, "over there."

"Listen, children, what does it say?"

"It says, 'Chic-a-chee, chic-a-chee,' over and over again," answered Jack.

"Pooh," interrupted Jimmie, "it says, 'Katy did, Katy didn't!'"

"It says, 'Katy broke a china plate; yes, she did; no, she didn't,'" called Betty.

"Yes, she did; no, she didn't!" the children shouted, merrily, together.

"Well," said the old man, "anyway, it's all about what Katy did do and what Katy didn't do. Probably Mr. Katy, like other good husbands in the world, is singing of the wonderful things Katy did do and the naughty things she didn't do. That is Mr. Katy's love-song. Ah, he finds Mrs. Katy very charming--her beautiful wings, her gracefully waving antenn? her knowing, shining eyes! Now, listen again. Katydid carries its musical instrument at the base of its wing cover. On each side is a tiny membrane and a strong vein. When the wing covers are rubbed together the membrane speaks, and you hear--"

"Katy did, Katy didn't!" shouted the children.

"Do you think you know where they are? Well, take these lanterns"--the guide had lighted half a dozen--"and find them."

The children scurried off, certain of a quick victory. In the woods about the cabin you could hear them shouting: "It's here!" "No, it isn't!" "Where is it?"

"A will-o'-the-wisp," murmured the old man; "may they never have a harder one to find!"

By-and-by the children came trotting back. They couldn't find the katydid in any place, and they had looked everywhere.

"Couldn't? How did you look?" He took one of the lanterns, went to a near-by tree, and held the lantern close to the leaves. "Here it is! Why, it's a great fellow!"

The children trooped into the cabin after him, crowding to look at the katydid.

"I thought they were brown," said Hope.

"So did I," echoed Betty.

"See, you can't tell this fellow from the leaf, it is such a bright, fresh green. Woe to the katydid if it were anything but this bright green! Just think how easily the birds would find them. What nice salad Katy would make for a young robin!"

"Do the birds eat katydids?" asked the children, in surprise.

"Oh yes, and they haven't any stated luncheon or supper time for doing it. They are very informal. One time is as good as another, and the oftener the merrier. If Katy doesn't keep very quiet and demure, like her leafy background, whist! and Father Robin or Mother Bluebird has a meal for the youngsters."

"Is that why it doesn't sing by day?" asked Peter.

"They wait till the birds go to bed, I suppose. See what a comical look this fellow has, waving its long, fine, silky antenn?about. Probably it's trying to find out what it is on, looking out for another nice green leaf to eat. They do a lot of damage eating leaves from the trees."

"What's that?" asked Betty, pointing to the edge of a leaf.

"Well, you have sharp eyes," said the old man. "Mrs. Katydid has laid her eggs there. See, the eggs are rounded and flattened, and each egg laps a little over the one in front of it. Once another man saw a row of katydid eggs laid as neatly as could be on the edge of a clean linen collar. I'll keep these eggs; then, in the spring, the young ones will hatch out. They will grow and shed their skins from time to time, just the way the locusts do. Ah, they leave so many old clothes about that they need an old clothes man! I wish I could tell you about the katydid I knew once upon a time who spent her days collecting old clothes, and how she made a fortune selling them to--"

Ben Gile paused and sighed deeply.

"Selling them to what?" shouted the children.

"I can't tell that to you," replied the old man, shaking his head sadly. "It's the story of 'How Katy Did.' I have to be very careful, for Mr. John Burroughs, who is a wiser old man than I am, says I mustn't. Lately the scientists almost killed one man I know, and a good, clever, useful man, for telling that story--very savage, very savage."

The children began to look troubled. "Will Mr. Burroughs hurt us?" inquired Hope. "My papa would--"

"No, no, child, you're too small. He likes something big, and he's especially fond of the Big Stick."

"Is that what he does his beating with?" Jack's eyes were frightened.

"He hunts with the Big Stick," answered the guide. "Dear me, where are we? It's half-past eight, and you children should have been in bed this time long, long ago. Hurry! Skip! Get the lanterns or we'll all be scolded."

And they scampered for the village, the guide driving them before him, and all the lights waving to and fro like so many crazy fireflies.

VI

FISHING

Have you ever started off on a bright, cool morning to fish? At the last it seems as if you would never get started, which, I suppose, is partly the eagerness to be gone; then you do get off, only to find you've forgot the can of worms or the salt for the luncheon-basket.

Jimmie and Betty were prancing on the lawn in front of Turtle Lodge. Jimmie had his camera over his back and a jointed steel rod done up in a neat little case in his hands, on his feet long rubber boots. Betty wore a big straw hat; she carried a little rod like Jim's and a pretty little knapsack, which held part of the luncheon. They were waiting for Jack and Ben Gile, who were to go with them to fish a stream that lay far back from the pond. It was to be a great day's sport. They had a creel and a rod for Jack; for the guide they needed to take nothing, for he had the most wonderful collection of rods and flies they had ever seen.

At last they saw him coming up the hill, Jack with him. Hastily they kissed Mrs. Reece, and ran shouting and jumping toward the old man and the boy, Lizzie after them, for they had left half the luncheon on the grass. "Faith!" she panted, catching up with them, "and what can you be doing without the victuals, I'd like to know?"

The guide took part of the bundles and Jack the rest. Off they went gayly talking and laughing.

Soon they were following the stream, Jack catching his line and fly in the alders almost every time he cast.

Jack was too poor ever to have had any rod except an alder stick cut beside the stream, a short line and hook, and any worm or grasshopper he might find. He was wonderfully proud of the rod he held. The children meant to give it to him at the end of the summer. But Jack did not know this good news yet.

Ben Gile led the way, and almost every time he cast his fly there was a swirl, the end of the slender rod bent, there was a minute of excitement, and then upon the bank lay a beautiful speckled trout. On, on, on they went over the cool, green leaves and bright red berries of the partridge vine, and past raspberries wherever the sun had struck in through the heavy trees to ripen them. The stream was running more and more swiftly as they travelled up grade; quick water was growing more frequent and the pools deeper.

At last they came to a deep, round pool, and the guide said, "Now, Jim, you've the first try."

Jimmie cast his fly, there was a strike, a plunge, and out, out, out ran Jimmie's line. The boy's face turned quite pale. "What shall I do, sir?"

"You have a big one," answered Ben, calmly. "If you can play him long enough we may get him; otherwise he'll get your fly and line. Steady there, steady; let out a little more line, and now reel in a bit."

It seemed like hours to Jimmie as he let the line out and reeled it in again. Really, it was only a few minutes before the guide said: "Seems to be getting a little tired; bring him in closer. That's it. There!"

They had no landing-net with them, so at the last moment Ben Gile seized the line, and out came a two-pound trout. Jimmie's eyes were popping nearly out of his head, and Betty was jumping about and clapping her hands.

"Tired?" asked the old man.

"Some," said the boy.

"Well, this is the best place we shall find to eat our luncheon. We'll camp here. Now for the fire! Boys, get the wood and a small strip of birch bark! Then these two stones will hold the frying-pan. Now for the fish; we'll keep that big one of yours and I'll mount it for you, if you'd like me to. We'll eat the little fellows. After luncheon we must catch more for your mother, Betty, and for Jack to take home with him."

Soon the frying-pan was hot, and the trout were sizzling and curling up with the bacon in the pan. Never did a luncheon taste so good as that, with fried trout and bacon, and hard-boiled eggs, soda biscuits, and a mammoth apple pie. They listened to the fire crackling; they looked up into the shining trees; they watched the water beyond the pool go tumbling downhill.

Finally the old man said, "It's going to be a clear day to-morrow."

The children gazed up into the sky.

At this Ben Gile laughed. "Don't look at the sky, look at your plates."

Puzzled by this, the children did look at their plates.

"But there's nothing left to look at," said Jack.

"That's just it. There's an old saying that people who eat all their food make a clear day for the morrow. Now," he continued, "I'll smoke my pipe of peace before we go on. Just look at that fellow darting about over the pool!"

"Oh!" cried Betty, "it's a darning-needle, and it will sew up my mouth and my eyes--oh, oh!"

"Nonsense, child, that's silly. The dragon-fly is a very useful and a very harmless fellow. It's a pity that there are so many superstitions about it."

"There's another name for it," said Jack--"devil's darning-needle."

"And in the South the darkies call it the mule-killer, and believe it has power to bring snakes to life. It's all nonsense. They are not only harmless to human beings but also very useful, for they eat flies and mosquitoes at a great rate. Once upon a time I fed a dragon-fly forty house flies in two hours. And they eat beetles and spiders and centipedes. And sometimes they eat one another."

"Like the crickets?" said Betty.

"Yes, like the crickets. Just see that fellow dart about. The sharpest sort of angles. There, it has something! It caught that lace-wing in its leg-basket."

"Leg-basket!" exclaimed the children.

"Yes; it draws its six legs together, and makes a sort of basket right under its head. Then the dragon-fly devours what it catches by these strong-toothed jaws. It is a hungry fellow, it is."

The old man puffed away quietly for a few minutes, while the children watched the darning-needle and hoped Ben Gile would say something soon.

"Those scientists," he continued, "who are working on flying-machines could learn a good deal from this fellow. The dragon-fly is made for flight. A long, slender, tapering body that cuts the air, moved by four narrow, gauzy wings, and steered by that pointed abdomen. They eat, mate, and lay their eggs while they are flying. I don't know that they are still for more than a few seconds."

"Can you find their eggs?" asked Betty.

"Yes; their eggs are laid in the water or fastened to the stems of water plants. See that damsel fly, the slender, smaller, pretty-colored darning-needle? Well, it goes entirely under water, cuts a slit in the stem with the sharp end of the abdomen, and lays the eggs in the groove it has made. And they lay thousands of eggs."

"When they hatch out, what do they look like?" asked Jack, who grew daily more interested in the creatures about him, and who, in the years to come, was destined to be a great scientist.

"It looks a little like the mother," said Ben Gile, taking out his pipe, "but not much. It goes through a great many changes before it is really grown up. All told, the growth takes from a few months to a whole year. The young one, called a nymph, is an ugly little fellow, dingy black with six sprawling legs, two staring eyes, and a big lower lip which covers up its cruel face like a mask. It is a true ogre, lurking under stones and in rubbish at the bottom of the pond seeking whom it may devour. It eats the smaller and weaker nymphs."

"Oh," said Betty, studying the picture the guide had drawn, "what an ugly, ugly fellow!"

"It changes its skin a good many times, and sometimes it looks a little better while the skin is still clean and light gray. But it soon turns dingy again. See these three little leaf-shaped gills I've drawn?"

"They are like the screw on a steamer," commented Jimmie.

"They are, a little. Well, this chap uses these gills for the same purpose as the steamer uses its screw--to scull through the water."

"What happens when it changes?" asked Jack.

"After the nymph has its full growth, some sunny morning soon after daylight, it makes its way up out of the water on to a stem and waits quietly for the old dark skin to split. Then out crawls a soft-skinned creature with gauzy wings. But the body is so moist and weak it has to wait awhile for the warm sunshine to harden the skin and strengthen the muscle. When this is done the new dragon-fly, with its glistening body, flies out from the pond in the bright, warm light."

"Then does it live forever?" asked Betty.

"No; it dies after twenty-five to forty-five days of Its flight. Here, Jack, catch that fellow!"

There was a wild scramble, but every time Jack just missed the dragon-fly. Finally Betty lent him her broad hat, and at last Jack caught the insect.

"Gee! aren't its eyes big?"

"And beautiful, too," said the guide. "They are made up of thousands of facets (a facet is just a small, plain surface) as many as thirty thousand facets in one eye. Some look up, some look down, some look out, some look in; so that there is nothing that escapes the sight of this hawk of the air. Look at the wings on this fellow, and look at the picture I drew for you of the nymph. Well, this fellow's wings begin in the nymph as tiny sacs, or pads, made by the pushing out of the wall of the body. Running all through between the two layers of the wing are thickened lines of chitin, which divide and subdivide, forming this fine network. In the new wing, protected by these thickenings, are air-tubes, which divide and branch into all parts of the wing. But as the wing reaches its full growth most of the air-tubes die." The guide paused.

"We are talking too much and fishing too little. Time to go on. Put out the fire, boys. Be sure that it's out. Run water all around it. Now we're off!" And up, up, up the brook they went.

VII

THE SWIMMING-POOL

Two or three days after the fishing expedition the boys had gathered together at the swimming-pool, Ben Gile with them. They had been racing, and climbing trees, and were very warm. "Come, boys," said the guide, "let's sit down a minute before you go into the water. It won't do to bathe when you're too warm. Look round on the stones under the water and see what you can find."

"Look at this," called Peter; "it's just like a sponge."

"It is a fresh-water sponge."

"I didn't suppose sponges grew in these parts at all," said Jimmie.

"Oh yes, there are many of them in the ponds."

"See this, sir," shouted Jack; "what funny little legs it has!"

"That's a May-fly or shad-fly nymph. He was hiding carefully under that stone and keeping out of the way of the dragon-fly nymph, who would so gladly gobble him up."

"It's prettier," said Jimmie, "than that dragon-fly nymph you drew a picture of."

"So it is. See, here on each side of its body are these fine little gill-plates, moving, moving, moving, so that they may get as much fresh air as possible out of the water. Each gill-plate is a tiny sac, and within these are the fine branches of the air-tubes. It's wonderful the way these creatures breathe."

"Don't they breathe just the way we do?" asked Jack.

"No; throughout the body of an insect is a system of tiny white tubes. Some day we'll look at these tubes under the microscope, and you will see that they are made up of rings. From end to end of the tube is a fine thread of chitin twisted in a close spiral like a spring. It is these little coils which look like rings. The coiled thread holds the little tube open so that the air may pass readily. But your little fellow, Jack, cannot have pores on the sides of the body like the last nymph. It lives under water, and the water would get into its tubes; instead, it has tracheal gills."

"That's a pretty big word," said Peter, looking up at the guide. He was growing impatient, and wished to begin the swim. If he had known what that swim was to mean to him, probably he would not have been so anxious.

"They aren't so hard to understand; they are just little oval sacs, inside of which is a limb of the air tube divided into tiny branches. The fresh air in the water passes through the thin wall of the gill and is taken by the air-tubes to all parts of the body, while the impure air passes out in the water. This is all that breathing means in any creature--a changing of impure for pure air."

"Then that is what my nymph is doing," asked Jack, "when it wiggles its gills so?"

"Just that. Your May-fly nymph, Jack, hatched from a tiny egg first. But it grows rapidly, and splits and sheds its skin sometimes as often as twenty times. During the last few months wings appear, which grow a little larger with each shedding of the skin. Finally, after three years--sometimes three years spent in growing and hiding away from its enemies--the little nymph floats up to the surface of the water. In a few minutes the old skin splits along the back, and from it flies forth a frail little May-fly. Its body is very soft and delicate. Its four wings are of a gauzy texture. At the tip of the body are two long, fine hairs. Its jaws are small and weak, but the life of this little creature is so short that it never eats. Up it flies into the air with thousands of its brothers and sisters, whirls in a mad dance for a few hours, then falls exhausted to the ground to die.

"Well, now I think we'd better go into the water," ended the guide. "You boys can go in just as you are." For three little boys had been sitting undressed in the bright sunshine. "Good for their pores," Ben Gile had told them, which is all very true.

Soon there was the greatest splashing and paddling and shouts of, "My goodness, isn't the water cold!" "Can you swim this way?" "How far can you go, anyway?"

Jimmie and the guide were swimming around near the shore when suddenly, two hundred feet ahead of them, they saw Peter disappear in what they supposed was shallow water. Jack was half-way the distance between the guide and Peter. It did not take him an instant to realize what had happened. But before he could get to the place where Peter had gone down, the lad had come up, struggled, and gone down again. As he came up once more Jack caught him by his curly hair, turned over on his back, holding Peter's head high out of the water, and swam calmly for the shallow place. Once there, the old man took Peter in his arms and hurried to shore, where they rolled him until they had the water out of him. Not a word was said, and modest, quiet Jack did not seem to think that he had been brave.

When Peter opened his eyes he said, "Guess my pores weren't in the right place."

VIII

THE RAINY DAY

It was a rainy day. Poor Betty flattened her little nose against the window-panes of Turtle Lodge a dozen times. But outside all she could see were just the long, straight lines of the down-coming rain and an empty road leading downhill to the edge of the pond; all she could hear was the drum of the water upon the roof. Inside, Jimmie was developing films in his laboratory, and was not in the least interested in what Betty might be doing.

"Oh, mother," called Betty, "I am so tired; there isn't anything to do!"

"Why don't you sew on a dress for Belinda?" asked Mrs. Reece.

"Belinda has too many clothes; she has more than I have, mother, and she's a naughty dolly to-day."

"Well, let me see--get Lizzie to let you make cake."

"Lizzie's cross, and I'm afraid to. I wish the guide were here. He's never cross, and never too busy to tell you something that's interesting." Betty looked out of the window. "He's coming now! Goody! Goody!"

When old Ben Gile reached the steps there was a little girl dancing inside the door and still shouting "Goody!"

"What's this?"

"You'll tell me a story, won't you?"

"Tell you a story! Dear, dear, I never knew such a little greedy for stories. I've brought you something."

Betty's face was shining now. She had forgotten the rain, the dreary day, cross Lizzie, and everything. Ben Gile took a box out of his pocket. "What is it?" she asked.

"I have a box full of little elves for you."

"Elves!" exclaimed Betty.

"Yes, little elves, little brownies."

"Come into the study, where there is a fire." Mrs. Reece led the way. "Then you can tell us all about these elves." They sat down around the fire, and Mrs. Reece continued, "Don't you think it would be fun to pop corn while we're hearing about the brownies?"

Betty was delighted, and ran for a corn-popper, and soon there was the merry sound of crackling wood, popping corn, and happy voices--all sounds that proved so tempting that before long Jimmie joined the others.

"My little elf is a bug," began the hermit.

"A bug an elf?"

"Yes, a bug; and when he doesn't look like an elf, he looks like a king with a high crown on his head or a naughty boy with a dunce cap."

"Let's see him, please," said Betty.

The old man opened his box. Inside lay a lot of little creatures with backs like beechnuts. "See, look through the lens!"

Betty laughed. "Oh, aren't they funny! The eyes are so big and so far apart."

"And the lines on their heads make them look as if they were gazing through heavy-bowed spectacles," said Mrs. Reece.

"There is a very wise man, and his name is Mr. Comstock, who says that Nature must have been in a joking mood when she made these little tree and leaf hoppers, they are so impish and knowing-looking. Ah, they are the naughty brownies of the insect world!"

"Betty, Betty," called Mrs. Reece, "your popcorn is burning!"

"Mother, I don't care to pop any more; let me just listen now. What makes them bad?"

"Well, they are born with a naughty desire to suck everything they can get their tiny sucking beaks upon. They hop around in great numbers on the fruit trees and pierce the leaves with their sharp beaks. Then, with a tubelike lower lip, they suck up the sap. They also make slits in the twigs in which to lay their eggs. In the following spring the eggs hatch, and there is a fresh supply of tree-hoppers ready to begin the mischief their parents left off only when they died."

"And what is the difference between the leaf-hoppers and the tree-hoppers?" asked Mr. Reece.

"Not much. They are cousins--cousins in naughtiness. The leaf-hoppers are a great nuisance. Every year they destroy from one-fourth to one-fifth of the grass that springs up. They also suck the sap of the rose, the grape-vine, and of many grains. These sturdy fellows live during the winter by hiding under the rubbish in the fields and vineyards, ready when the warm spring does come to begin their naughty work."

"What makes a little fellow like this able to do so much damage?" asked Jimmie, who had come in, his hands all stained with chemicals.

"Well, it is well covered by this horny substance called chitin, and then it is very active. You see, the chitin acts both as armor-plate for the soft parts and also as a firm support to the many muscles. As many as two thousand separate, tiny muscles have been counted in a certain caterpillar. That shows how very active insects are."

"And they all have such big eyes they can see everything," said Betty.

"So they have--bigger eyes than the old wolf of the story had."

"You remember, I told you about the thousands of facets in the big eyes of the darning-needle? Not contented with these large eyes, most insects have three small eyes arranged in the form of a triangle on the front of the head."

"This bug has feelers, too," said Jimmie.

"So it has. Insects use these feelers, or antenn? for all sorts of purposes-- some for touch, some for smell, some for hearing. Ants exchange greetings by touching antenn? and recognize a friend or an enemy by the odor. The antenn?of a male mosquito are covered with fine hairs. When Mrs. Mosquito sings, all the tiny hairs on Mr. Mosquito's feelers are set in motion, and he becomes aware of Mrs. Mosquito."

Mrs. Reece laughed. "That's a new kind of romance!"

"Mother, what's a romance?" asked Betty.

"You'll know, dear, in time."

"Notice this imp's mouth," said the guide. "It's made for sucking. But there's a great difference in the mouths of insects: some are made for biting, some for lapping, some for piercing, and some for sucking. The butterfly, which lives on nectar in the depths of the flowers, has a long, coiled tube which scientists call a proboscis. This it unrolls and buries in the throat of the flower. Mrs. Mosquito has a file and pump, for it is she, and not her husband, who does all the singing and biting. The male mosquito has nothing more than a mouth for sucking nectar. And I told you about the biting jaws of the locust with which it nibbles grass and leaves."

"And does the tree-hopper breathe the way the locust does--through those pores on the side?"

"Yes, child," said the old man, "and the air-pores are protected by fine hairs which surround the openings, just the way the hairs in your nostrils keep the dust from getting up your nose and into your throat."

"Things in the bugs," said Betty, "are so like us."

"The world becomes more and more like one great whole as you grow older," added Ben Gile. "Those are interesting elves I've been telling you about, aren't they?"

"I didn't know bug elves could be so interesting."

"Now run and get us some of the fresh cake Lizzie has been baking," said Mrs. Reece. "I hope it will taste as good as it smells."

IX

THE PRIZE

There were two canoes going up the little river which led out from the pond. In the first were Ben Gile with Betty, Hope, and Jack. In the second Jimmie and Peter paddled Mrs. Reece. They had trout rods, although they did not plan to fish very much, and well-filled luncheon-baskets, magnifying-glasses, cameras, boxes, and various other things.

In two weeks they were to go on a camping expedition, and to-day's trip was taken chiefly to find a good place for the first night's stop.

The children were all excitement about the camping, which was to be the last jollity of their happy summer, and they asked so many questions about what they were to take with them, and they asked the same questions over so many times, that at last Mrs. Reece put her hands on her ears and called to the guide, who was paddling vigorously ahead.

"Well," he called back, "a frying-pan and an axe, and perhaps a tent." He allowed his canoe to drop nearer Mrs. Reece's. "What naughty children you are," he continued, "to bother the life out of your poor mother! I know of some other children, too, who are very naughty. I see one flying now."

"That pretty little thing," exclaimed Betty, "with the gauzy wings?"

"Yes, that pretty little thing; its wings have many, many veins. When Lace-Wing is a baby and is called a larva, it does not look like this, for its jaws are strong and very sharp. After it has eaten and grown for some time it makes a house for itself, where it rolls up for a nap. While it is lying very still in this little house many things are happening."

"What happens?" asked Jack.

"Well, it is changing from a baby to a grown-up, and while it is growing up into an insect it is called a pupa. Don't mistake this for papa--it does not look like your papa at all."

Betty thought this was very funny, because her father was a great big man over six feet tall.

"After its wings are made and it looks just like its mamma, Lace-Wing crawls out of its house and flies away."

[Illustration: Pit of the Ant-Lion]

"Has it any cousins, like the locust?" asked Betty.

"Yes, it has cousins; the ant-lion and caddis-fly both belong to this family. But little Lace-Wing, with its beautiful green body, gauzy wings, and golden eyes, is the most graceful member of the family."

"How do they live when they are babies?" asked Hope.

"When they are babies," said Ben Gile, opening his eyes wide and speaking in a loud, deep voice, "they go about like lions seeking whom they may devour."

Betty was frightened.

"No, no, child," said Mrs. Reece, "not a real lion."

"Just an aphis-lion," explained the guide, his eyes twinkling. "They are called aphis-lions because they are very cruel to the little green plant-lice I told you about. You remember, the plant-lice live on plants, and with their sucking beaks pump the sap from the plants. The aphis-lions crawling over the plants come across the little aphid. Quick as a wink they stick their sharp claws in the soft body of the plant-louse and drink the blood with their sharp-pointed jaws. They are very fond of eggs, too, and Mamma Lace-Wing is careful of her eggs, because she knows the mischievous ways of her children."

"What does Mamma Lace-Wing do with her eggs?" inquired Mrs. Reece.

"Each egg which she lays has a tiny stem, and the stems are fastened to a leaf or twig. When the babies hatch out they crawl down onto the leaf and hunt around for something to eat. Perhaps if they knew more they would crawl up the little egg stems and eat their own brothers and sisters."

"Oh, what cannibals!" cried Betty.

"Yes, it is not pleasant, this Fiji Island of the insects, but it is their nature."

"They do seek their meat from God," murmured Mrs. Reece.

"Yes, it is a mystery," answered the old man. "But, dear me, I have forgotten my story. Well, in about ten days they find a nicely sheltered spot and spin a little silken cocoon about themselves. In this they stay for a couple of weeks, while they are changing into grown-up lace-wings. When they are finished they cut a round door in their silken house, spread their gauzy wings, stretch their delicate green bodies, rub their eyes in wonder at the sunny world, and fly away to lay some little eggs on slender stems just like those which their mothers laid and from which they came."

"See," said Jimmie, "what a place for camping!"

"But it is too near home," objected Peter. "We could get here in two hours."

"So we could," admitted Jimmie.

"Tell us something about the cousins, sir," said Jack.

"We can't have much more now," replied the guide, "for we shall have to stop for luncheon soon. But I'll tell you about a little fellow called the ant-lion. Along the side of almost any country path or road, if you keep your eyes open, you may notice some day little pits of sand with sloping sides, and down at the bottom of this is a hole. The hole is very dark, and unless you look sharply you will think it just a hole. But if you examine it you will see a little head and two little sharp, curved jaws. These are the jaws of the ant-lion, lying in wait to gobble up the first passer-by. The rest of the body is in a little tunnel burrowed out in the sand. They get their name, I suppose, because they think an ant an excellent dinner. They lie there knowing very well that Mr. and Mrs. Ant will surely slip on the steep-sloping sides. And if by any chance they don't, these ant-lions have been seen to throw up sand with their heads in order to hit a helpless little ant and knock it down into the pit."

The children exclaimed at this cleverness.

"After it has eaten its fill, this cruel, greedy fellow makes a little room for itself of fine grains of sand firmly held together with silky fibres. In this room it lies quietly, sometimes all winter, until it changes into a grown-up ant-lion with four long, narrow wings. Then Mrs. Ant-Lion lays her eggs in the sand, and when the young ones hatch out they build the 'pits of destruction' which I told you about. What book is it, children, that uses the 'pit of destruction' so often as a figure?"

"The Bible!" shouted Peter, who was the minister's son in Rangeley Village.

"Good! Now, no more for the present, and here we are at a splendid place for luncheon--clear spring, dry ground, handy wood, and all."

The canoe beached noiselessly on the river's edge, the boys jumped out with a whoop, and soon luncheon and frying-pans were out of the canoes, and there was the sound of the axe chopping the dry wood, the good smell of smoke, and the sizzling of bacon. Betty and Hope went for water. The boys fetched wood. Mrs. Reece and the guide took care of the luncheon, Mrs. Reece spreading the table on the ground, and the guide frying the potatoes and bacon.

"Oh, mother," said Jimmie, "what does make things taste so good out-of-doors?"

"I'm sure I don't know."

"And, mother," asked Betty, "what does make everything so pretty?"

"You ask mother a hard question."

"And oh, Mrs. Reece," exclaimed Jack, his thin, eager face shining with excitement, "everything in the world is so wonderful!"

"It's all so different in the winter," said Peter, in between bites of bread-and-butter. "It isn't half so nice, but I suppose it would be lovely if we could have you and Mr. Gile--"

"You dear child!"

"It is about three miles above here," the guide spoke, "on the last of the Dead River Ponds, where we shall find our first camping ground. I want you to look at it."

"And we'll be gone days and days."

"Goody! goody!" called Betty, clapping her hands. "And we'll sleep out-of-doors, cook out-of-doors, and do everything out-of-doors."

Every one smiled with her, for there was not a person there who was not looking forward with happiness to this trip.

"Before we start on I'll smoke my pipe," said the old man.

"Then, please, sir, won't you tell us something else?" asked Betty.

"Why, I have nothing left in my head, you child."

"Oh, please, sir, you said there was another cousin called the caddis-worm."

"So I did," said the old man. "Fetch me that stone, Jack." He pointed to a stone lying in the water. Jack brought it to him, and he broke something off from it. "What's that?"

"That's a stick," answered Betty.

"No, that's not a stick, that's a caddis-worm. This little fellow, unlike some spoiled children I know, has to find its own dinner, change its own clothes, tuck itself into bed, and build its own house. And it is brighter than some children I know," said the old man, looking kindly at Peter. "The caddis-worm builds itself different kinds of houses. Some of the houses are shaped like the horns you blow on the Fourth of July, and one kind of house is made of the finest sand, fastened together with bands of finest silk, which the caddis spins. Our caddis-worm has patience," said the old man, shaking his head and looking at Jimmie--"patience, plenty of patience." He puffed away at his pipe for a few seconds. "Some build rougher houses, choosing small pebbles instead of sand. Of these it builds a long tube. Others make a little green summer cottage with twigs, grasses, and pine-needles, from which they build an attractive bungalow by laying down four pieces and crossing the ends like this: # These cottages are built about an inch long, and in them the young caddis-worms have a cool and cosey summer home. Often these little houses have silken hangings inside. The little owners fasten the hooks at the ends of their bodies to these and moor themselves securely."

"What do you call it a worm for?" asked Mrs. Reece.

"Well, it looks a little like a worm. It has a long, slender body, but it has six jointed legs, which real worms don't have. See this fellow!" Ben Gile pulled the worm out of its case.

"Oh, see! part of the body is so pale and soft!"

"That, child, is because it is always covered by the little house. The front end and the legs, however, are darker. That's sunburn, I suppose."

"When young Master Caddis-Worm goes out for a swim or a walk it pushes its six legs out-of-doors, and walks along, carrying its house with it. Very convenient, you see! No doors to lock! And if it gets tired it does not have to walk home; it just walks in and goes to sleep under a nice, smooth stone. Some roam about and some stay at home. These creatures are pretty much like human beings in their ways.

"One of the young caddis-worms prefers fishing to walking, like some other young fellows I know. On a stone near its house it spins a fine web, turned up-stream, so that any tender little insects floating down-stream get lodged in it. An easy way to get your dinner--just to go to a net and eat."

The guide paused for a long time, clouds of smoke circling about his white beard and white hair. The children thought he would never go on. "I've had something on my mind for days," he said, "and I'll speak of it now. The boy or girl who learns most about the ants before September 15th shall win a prize. This prize is to be a magnifying-glass, a book of colored plates of the insects, very beautiful and very big, and a five-dollar gold piece."

"A prize, a prize!" shouted the children, jumping madly about, while Mrs. Reece and the guide smiled at each other.

"Now we've had our dinner, our rest, our pipe of peace, a plan for a prize, and we must push on for the camping-ground. Get the canoes ready."

And, with laughter and talking, the canoes were off up the river again.

X

A NAGGING FAMILY

"Do you know of a family around here whom no one likes?" asked Ben Gile.

The lanterns were burning brightly out on the lawn of Turtle Lodge, and Mrs. Reece had just stopped playing so that the children might rest from dancing. All the lanterns moved gently to and fro on the piazza; the children were running about, and everybody seemed to be having a beautiful and breathless time. "Do you know of a family around here," called the guide, "whom nobody likes?"

"I do," replied Mrs. Reece, laughing and slapping the side of her face. "They are just like some people, nagging, annoying, and numerous."

"Do any children here," called Ben Gile, for the third time, "know of a family nobody likes? For the child who guesses I have a pocket-knife."

"The Smiths!" shouted Peter. "My father says Mrs. Smith is always quarrelling with the choir."

"Hush!" said Mrs. Reece, seeing danger ahead. "Ben means a family right here on the piazza."

The children looked at one another, and then Jack turned shrewdly to the guide. "I guess, sir, it is mosquitoes and flies."

"Good boy, and here's the knife."

Jack thought he had never seen such a wonderful knife. It had three blades, a corkscrew, a file, and a pair of scissors, and to this day Jack has that knife.

"Come," said Mrs. Reece, "let us all sit down for a few minutes while Lizzie is getting supper ready inside."

"How many wings," asked Mrs. Reece, "has a fly?"

"Four," answered Jimmie.

"No," corrected the guide; "a real fly has only two wings. In the place of the second pair they have queer little knobbed rods which are called balancers-- something like the out-riggers on your scull, Jim. These steer and steady the fly's body."

"What makes a fly bite?" asked Hope.

"They do not bite, child. A beetle or a grasshopper can really bite, because beetles and grasshoppers have heavy, horny jaws, toothed on the edge, with which to do it. But a fly has fine, sharp-pointed jaws. With these needlelike jaws they pierce a hole in the skin, then with a tiny sucking-beak, made by the rolled lower lip, they draw up the blood through this opening."

"I wonder whether any little girl here knows why flies should not be allowed in the house?" asked Mrs. Reece. No little girl did know anything except that their mothers were always driving flies out, and that these creatures buzzed and were a nuisance. "Do tell them," said Mrs. Reece.

"Well," said the guide, "the fly is such a little acrobat it can crawl up the steepest and most slippery wall and walk upside down or right side up with the greatest ease. Perhaps some day you can make a fly keep still long enough so that you can look at its foot. At the end of the foot are two little round pads thickly covered with downy hair. On each side are two sharp claws and many stiff, clinging hairs. With this flattened foot it can go wherever it wishes.

"But this same little foot is the chief reason why a fly should never be allowed in the house, for flies crawl into all sorts of dirty places, and the fine hairs catch and hold the dirt. When the fly lights on us or on the table, some of the pieces of dirt are shaken off."

"But they are so hard to catch," said Betty; "it takes Lizzie forever and forever to get them out of the dining-room in the morning."

"I know why they are hard to catch," added Jack, "for I've looked at a dead fly. They have such big eyes, like lighthouses, they can see all around."

"Yes," said Ben Gile; "there is no such thing as creeping up on a fly unawares. Flies are dirty creatures," continued the old man, "and the time is not very far distant when people will make war on them just as they do on mosquitoes. Mrs. Fly lays her eggs in unclean places, and as many as a hundred eggs at a time. These eggs hatch out quickly. It takes only twenty-one days to make a chicken out of an egg, but to make a baby fly it takes only a few hours, and ugly babies they are--little white maggots, or worms, that live and feed and grow rapidly in dirty places. Within six days the maggot becomes a tiny, dark-brown pupa, and after five days the pupa hatches out into a grown-up fly."

A dozen little girls at the party made up their minds promptly that after this evening they, at least, would make war on flies.

"And aren't flies of any use?" asked Betty.

"There is one little fly, Mrs. Tachina-Fly, who is of some use. She is a cousin of the house-fly. She is of use because she chooses a queer place to lay her eggs--on the back of a young caterpillar. After these caterpillars grow and shut themselves up into a cocoon to change into a butterfly the little fly eggs hatch out into maggots. Of course they are hungry--all babies are; and finding the nice, fat caterpillar in the round house, like dutiful babies they eat what is set before them until the fat, tender caterpillar is eaten up. After they are satisfied they lie still in their brown skins and change into grown-up tachina-flies, and at last out come a lot of busy, buzzing, bothersome flies. It is rather hard on the caterpillar. But when we think what harmful, greedy things most caterpillars are, perhaps it is good that there are tachina-flies to eat them. Is it time for supper yet?"

"No, not yet," replied Mrs. Reece. "Do tell the children something about mosquitoes."

"If I had to choose between Mr. and Mrs. Mosquito, I should take Mr. Mosquito, for he neither bites nor buzzes, but attends strictly to his own business. Perhaps he thinks Mrs. Mosquito's voice pretty. Perhaps he likes to hear about her adventures. But most people do not, for they think Mrs. Mosquito a busybody, always going where she is not wished, always breaking up conversations, and always coming back after she has been plainly told that she is not wanted. Yet her singing is music in the ears of her husband. Perhaps if we had long, slender antenn? all covered with hairs, like his, we, too, might like her song. When she sings these hairs begin to tremble, to vibrate, and a little nerve in the antenn?changes this trembling to sound.

"In every way Mr. Mosquito seems a more pleasant body. He eats very little, and contents himself with nectar. But she, knowing that excitement makes the blood flow faster, and being a hearty eater, begins her song gently at first, then louder and louder, nearer and nearer. Finally, with her long, slender, sharp stylets, she makes a hole in your cheek or your arm, pushes in her sucking-beak, and pumps up the blood. And there she sucks and sucks until her stomach is full or she is brushed off or killed."

"Where do mosquitoes lay eggs?" asked Jack, who was certain that everything in the insect world did lay eggs, as indeed everything does.

"In the water; any puddle will do. When the eggs hatch out they are funny-looking fellows, long, tapering bodies with a big head end. At the other end are two little prongs. This baby, like some other babies, is never quiet, but squirms and wriggles so that it is called a wriggler. Upon its thick head are two little tufts of hair. These it waves every moment, so that all the food which comes its way will go into its hungry little mouth. One of the prongs at the other end of the body is an air-tube, so that the baby mosquito has to stand on its head to breathe. It hangs head downward, and holds its air-tube above the surface of the water.

"When people pour kerosene upon the water the wriggler cannot get any air to breathe, and therefore dies. Within a few days the wriggler changes its skin three times; after the third change it looks very different, and is called a pupa. Now, instead of having an air-tube at the end, it has two on the back of the thorax. At the tail end are two flaps to help it swim. Even the pupa is never still a minute, but holds its air-tubes above the water's surface.

"When anything comes to disturb it, it uses its flaps and swims safely to the bottom of the pool. At the end of two days out of the pupa skin comes a grown-up mosquito. If it is a Mrs. Mosquito, she promptly begins to bite people and to carry about fevers or malaria from person to person. The bite of a mosquito may sometimes be as dangerous as the bite of a rattlesnake."

The children had been slapping the mosquitoes buzzing about on the piazza. "And now," said the guide, "before we go into supper, I will tell you a real and a true story. Mosquitoes sometimes carry sickness from one person to another until it spreads throughout a large city. We didn't realize how dangerous mosquitoes were till a short time ago. People had malaria, and were very ill with it. In some countries many died. Every one thought, however, that the malaria came in some mysterious way from the mists of the low-lying swamps and marshes. But one day some one happened to think it might not be in the marshes, after all; rather that it might be a certain little two-winged insect with a short, piercing instrument, which spent its babyhood days in these same marshes.

"And so two English doctors determined to find out the truth of the matter. In the faraway land of Italy was a place where thousands of people were suffering from this disease. There these doctors went and built a comfortable little house in the very worst place they could find. They were careful to screen every door and window, and to leave not a crack for a mosquito to crawl in.

"There they lived, always going into the house at sundown, shutting all the screen doors, but allowing the damp night air to pour in. It was this night air which every one supposed gave people malaria. But the two physicians in the snug little house, free from mosquitoes, kept well, strong, and happy, although the people outside in the other houses were very ill and suffering with chills and fever.

"You see, these little Anopheles, for that is their name, bite some one ill with malaria. Perhaps the next person they stab with their sharp needle is well. In this way they leave some of the poisoned blood in the wound. There is another illness which is a hundred times worse than malaria. This is called yellow fever. In some countries thousands of people died from this every year, and doctors did not know just how it was carried from place to place.

"Our Government appointed a commission to study the matter. Dr. Walter Reed, a surgeon of the United States Army, with three assistants, went to Havana and built a house, carefully screened, just like that of the English physicians in Italy. People thought that the fever was carried in the clothes and on the sheets of those who were ill. To prove that this was not so, these men wore the clothes of sick people, and even slept on the sheets taken from the sickbed. They did this disagreeable thing for twenty days, keeping the little house very warm, and shutting out the fresh air and sunshine. But in spite of all these things the men continued well and strong.

"They wanted to prove even more surely that it was a certain kind of mosquito which really did the harm. So they built another house. Everything in this house was pure and clean. The rooms were flooded with fresh air and sunshine. Half of the house was carefully screened and shut off from the other half. The men in the half that was screened kept perfectly well. Those in the other half let themselves be bitten by mosquitoes which had been in the houses where there was yellow fever. All became dangerously ill with the fever. Two of these brave physicians died of the fever while trying to find the cause, in order that they might save the lives of thousands of people."

"That is modern heroism," said Mrs. Reece, "and service of the highest sort. All humanity is indebted to those brave men. There is no doubt but that our Panama Canal could not be in progress to-day were it not for the extermination of the mosquito in the canal zone. Since we can never tell where a mosquito has been, or what kind of a mosquito it is, I suppose it is best to keep mosquitoes from biting, and always to keep them out of the house. And now, children, supper is ready, and after that games. Let us go to the dining-room!"

XI

CAMPING OUT

At last the day, expected all summer long, had come. The children, Hope and Betty, Jack, Peter, and Jimmy, Mrs. Reece and Ben Gile, were gathered on the edge of the pond, their packs in the canoes, their paddles at bow and stern. Other guides had taken the food and tents ahead the day before. Their friends had gathered to bid them good-bye, and finally, amid the farewells, they were off, Jimmie in a canoe by himself, Jack and Peter paddling Mrs. Reece, and Ben Gile with the two little girls. Everybody was so excited that all talked at once, and nobody could hear any one else. Hope and Betty had never been camping before, and the boys meant to show the girls all the wonders of sleeping and eating out in the woods.

Finally they came to a "carry"--that is, a path leading from one lake to another, across which the food and canoes have to be lugged. The girls and Mrs. Reece carried the packs and food over, making several trips in order to do so; and the boys and the guide, crossing their paddles under the thwarts of the canoes and raising the blades on their shoulders, balanced the canoes and trotted swiftly over the carry. Nothing seemed any trouble that glorious, beautiful day--nothing too heavy, nothing too hard. Betty and Hope could have skipped over every inch of the trail, and they were quite sure that they could have done all the paddling, too. And Betty did learn, in after years, not only to paddle, but also to carry her own canoe, for she grew to be a big, strong, athletic girl, with rosy cheeks and a quick, sure step.

Hour after hour they went from one pond to another. The ponds were larger and wilder at each crossing, and already they were in a wilderness of woods and lakes, and heard the whistle of the hawk, the scream of the lonely eagle, and the crazy cries of the loon. Every once in a while a big heron mounted lazily upward and flew off solemnly to a place where his peace need not be disturbed.

[Illustration: A. Moth. B. Caterpillar. C. Side view of head of moth. D. and E. Scales from the wing of a butterfly.]

Although Hope and Peter and Jack lived all the year around in Rangeley Village, yet they had never been so far away from home before, and to them it seemed very wonderful. Even in the midst of it all, however, Jack did not forget the prize Ben Gile had offered. He hurried over carry after carry, and at the end of each one might be found flat on his face studying some little hill of ants.

At last, after travelling five hours, they came to a halt, ravenously hungry. Dinner was cooked and eaten, and then, after dinner, they began their long ascent of Saddleback, for they were going to a lonely little pond on the second highest mountain in the State of Maine. There, at Camp-in-the-Clouds, was a cabin in which Mrs. Reece could sleep, and the girls, too, if they wished, although they declared that they would not.

Up, up the hill they trudged, stepping over blow-downs, following their footing carefully, and watching with interest the little animals that scampered out of their way. But never did packs grow so heavy, and at last Mrs. Reece, who was carrying nothing but Jack's camera, sat down panting and laughing.

"I can't go a step farther," she declared, "until I catch my breath."

"This is a good place to rest," assented the guide. "Some deer found it so this morning, I think. Here, catch that butterfly, Jack!"

In a flash Jack had caught the butterfly, and brought it, gently, to Ben Gile.

"You don't see this fellow up here often. Who knows the difference between a butterfly and a moth? No one? Well, that is because most children are going to bed about the time the moth begins to fly. Doesn't any one know? You have all seen moths and butterflies? Well, well, well!

"The first thing you see is that when the moth lights on the edge of a flower-cup, instead of holding the wings up above the body, as the butterfly does, it spreads its wings flat over the body. Then a butterfly has little knobs at the tips of its slender antenn? while the moth has slender ones without knobs, or pretty, feathery ones that look like plumes."

"I supposed," said Peter, "that moths and butterflies were just the same, except that moths will fly into the house and burn their wings on the lamps." Peter didn't in the least care about moths and butterflies. He was longing to get to the top of the mountain, but he was too polite to seem impatient.

"They are alike in many ways. You remember, do you not, that the locust has a pair of soft jaws covering over the dark, hard ones? In the moths and butterflies these jaws are different. Each one is long, and has a deep groove on the inner side. These two grooves fit together, and make a slender tube called a proboscis. When flying this long tube is rolled up in a tight coil under the head; alighting, the proboscis is quickly uncoiled and dipped into the throat of the flower, and the sweet nectar sipped from it. See here, Jack, what have you on your fingers?"

"The dust from the butterfly's wings, sir."

"No, not quite dust, or powder, either. That dust is tiny hair and scales. If I had a powerful lens in my pocket I could show you how deeply some of these tiny scales are scalloped, so that they look like a hand with fingers. If you rubbed all the scales off that wing there would be no color left, for the scales are like little sacs, and many of them contain grains of color called pigment-- red, yellow, or brown. You have all seen the rainbow of colors on a soap-bubble? Well, the brilliant colors of the wing are made in just the same way as the colors on a bubble: by the light striking the little ridges on the overlapping scales."

"It is not only we who are fearfully and wonderfully made," said Mrs. Reece, "but even the tiniest creatures God has created, and all with a purpose, all with a place."

The guide nodded his head. "The more you study, the more you see how every least thing is part of a great mysterious whole. If you look at a butterfly's wing from which the scales have been rubbed you will see plan and purpose in the placing of even those scales; for the little pits into which the stems of the scale fit are turned all one way, toward the base of the wing."

"They are so beautiful!" exclaimed Betty. "Are they always pretty?"

"That depends," replied the old man, "whether in their caterpillar youth you think them pretty. They have a bad name, then, for being homely, and do a good deal of damage."

"Oh, I hate caterpillars!" cried Hope.

"Fuzzy caterpillars hump so and crawl," said Betty.

"You mean woolly bears?"

"Woolly bears!" exclaimed the children.

"Yes; not Teddy bears. They have to play somehow, so they wiggle for joy, and this takes them along very fast--that is, fast for a caterpillar. Sometimes they spin a long thread by which they take a flying short cut and land--on your back."

Jimmie dropped a tiny twig down Betty's back, which made her scream.

"But they don't harm us," said Ben Gile. "They are so fussy about what they eat for dinner that they wouldn't think of biting even the sweetest little boy or girl. They prefer something far more tender. Ah, you wouldn't like Isabella!" The old man shook his head sadly.

"Isabella! Who is Isabella?" questioned the children.

"Isabella is always in a hurry," said the guide--"always. She is brown in the middle, and black on the head and tail end, Isabella is, and she walks rapidly, as if she had a great deal to do before she could take time to be made over into a tiger-moth. She stops every once in a while to make sure she is on the right road; then she hurries along in a nervous, fidgety way, looking for a nice, comfortable stone under which to have a winter home, for Isabella is in such haste that she could never think of taking time to spin a cocoon."

"But do all caterpillars turn into moths or butterflies?" asked Jack.

"Yes, every one, my son, that lives long enough, just as surely as a boy will turn into a man. The butterfly lays the egg, and after the egg has been quiet for a while out comes a little worm; the worm spins the cocoon, and out of the cocoon comes a perfect moth, or butterfly. It is a wonderful cycle, a wonderful series of changes. Little boys and girls seem to be surrounded with more love and don't change their skins as moths do, but the mystery of life belongs quite as much to the helpless moth as it does to any one of us."

"But is a caterpillar an insect, and is a butterfly an insect?" asked Betty.

"Of course, you goose," said Jimmie; "you don't expect to hatch a duck from a hen's egg, do you?"

But Ben Gile, who was older than Jimmie and decidedly more patient, explained, carefully: "If you look at a caterpillar and a moth you will see that their bodies aren't so unlike, after all. They are made up of rings, and both the moth and the caterpillar have six legs apiece. Most caterpillars have little prop legs, but these aren't real legs and shouldn't be counted. Caterpillars eat and eat and eat; they are such solid little chaps they must need a good many legs, real and false, to keep moving at all. Well, heigho! stretch your own legs, boys! We'll leave the caterpillar where it is, and move on to the top of the mountain, or we'll never be there in time to eat our own supper. One, two, three, march!"

And off they went, talking and laughing and scrambling up the side of the mountain, which swung dark and steep above them.

XII

CAMP-IN-THE-CLOUDS

The camp was reached. Once there, the children found the other two guides in the cabin. The cook-tent was already pitched; the sleeping-tents had been left so that the boys might choose their own locations and help in pitching them. It was a beautiful place--remote, wild, two-thirds up the side of the great mountain.

In front was the famous trout pond, and beyond the little valley made by the pond the crest of the mountain rose higher and higher. Dusk was coming on, and the crisp mountain air was filled with the shadows of the woods; along the mountain summit lay streamers of white cloud. Down, down, down reached the long fingers of cloud, and up, up, up reached the deep shadows, just as if a great hand were closing the world in dusk. Every little sound was as clear in the evening air as the water of the pond was transparent. Small shadows moved about the edge of the pond--deer, they were, said Ben Gile, that had come down to the edge to drink.

"Phew, isn't it cold!" shouted the children, as they ran from one thing to another; "and won't supper taste good!"

Jack, who hadn't on any stout boots like Jimmie's, and whose jacket was threadbare and thin, began to think the sleeping-blankets would feel good when it was time to crawl in. In front of the cabin blazed a big camp-fire, and around this fire supper was served. "Did stewed apricots, soda-biscuits, bacon, eggs, hot cakes, ever taste so good? Will they ever taste so good again? Did hot cakes and syrup ever make the butter fly so fast?" asked Ben Gile.

"And, speaking of the butterfly," he went on, "it's not time to turn in yet, it's too dark to fish or explore, so let me tell you a little more about the butterfly, and if you don't like it you can just imagine it is a hot-cake butterfly."

The children thought this was a great joke. But Peter, who had eaten so much he was almost asleep, didn't hear what Ben Gile said.

"Well," the old man continued, just as if he were beginning where he had left off in the afternoon--"well, the caterpillar eats so much--it eats almost as much as Peter does"--at this Peter opened his eyes good-naturedly--"it eats so much that very soon it grows too big for its skin, so the old skin splits for the growing body, and out comes young caterpillar in a clean, new dress--a very easy way for Mrs. Butterfly to have her babies get new clothes. Don't you think it is, Mrs. Reece?--no hems to stitch, no buttons to sew on, no darning. The only things their mothers ever do for them is to start them with the food they like.

"And such a butterfly this mother is that little she cares whether her children are considered pests or not, because they eat everything green that they like, and eat before they are invited. A long sigh of relief the gardener or farmer draws when the caterpillars lie quiet to pupate. They lie very, very quiet, with wings, antenn? and legs folded under the body."

"What does pupate mean?" asked Betty, who was poking the fire and listening hard to every word the old man spoke.

[Illustration: A. Cocoon of a polyphemus moth. B. Cocoon of a cecropian moth.]

"It means just that--to lie quiet and change. They do it in different ways. Some crawl down into the ground and some pull out their silky hairs, and with these and the silk they can spin they make a soft, silken cocoon. Some make over their last skin into a hard covering. The monarch butterfly does this.

"And there is a troublesome creature called the clothes moth--Mrs. Reece can tell you about that--who lays its eggs on anything woollen it can find. After a while a baby clothes moth, a whitish worm, hatches out. Then this little fellow eats the fibres of the wool, and finally spins a cocoon out of these fibres and its own silk.

"Some caterpillars are leaf-rollers--that is, when they pupate they roll over the corners of a leaf, make themselves a neat hammock, and there lie quite still in a cool and comfortable place to sleep."

Poor Peter had tumbled over, his head on Mrs. Reece's lap. Betty and Hope, wide awake, were thinking just as much of the wonderful tent in which they were to sleep as of the butterflies and moths. They were wide awake enough to point their fingers at sleepy Peter.

"I think there is one kind of moth," said Mrs. Reece, stroking Peter's silky hair, "that spins something almost as soft as this."

"Softer," affirmed Ben Gile; "and that is the silk-worm."

"Does the caterpillar make the silk our dresses are made from?" asked Betty.

"Yes, indeed. The mother moth is a creamy-white. She lays several hundred eggs; from each of these eggs comes a little worm. These little worms have been cared for so long by men that they don't know how to take care of themselves any more.

"They like to eat the leaves of the mulberry-tree. If these leaves are not to be found they will sometimes eat lettuce. For forty-five days they eat as fast as they can, which is a good deal faster than greedy children can eat.

"Every ten days or so they cast aside their old skin and come out in a new one. After the last moulting of the skin the worm begins to spin a cocoon about itself. At first the cocoon is not very smooth, but in a while the worm gets well started and spins the rest of it with one long, silky thread."

"Isn't that wonderful!" exclaimed one of the guides. "I suppose that silk is finer than the finest trout-line."

"A hundred times finer," answered Ben. "Usually it is three hundred yards long. Before the pupa has a chance to make its way out, and so destroy the long, silken thread, the man who has taken such care of the worm drops the cocoon into boiling water, which kills the pupa at once. Then the precious silk thread is carefully unwound on to little spools, and is ready to be made into thread or spun into silk.

"And now, children, it's time for you to spin your dreams. Shake up Peter, and we'll get ready for the night. Too bad to leave this fire, but we can have one as often as we want."

The boys slept like tops, but there were two little girls who lay rather wide awake most of the night, listening to the strangest grunting sounds in the world.

XIII

STORM-BOUND

After two glorious days of exploring--"exploricating," the guides called it-- the children went to bed early, expecting to make an early start to hunt partridge. They were so tired from their good times that for two or three hours they slept like tops.

But in front of the cabin Ben Gile and Mrs. Reece and the other guides were looking at the night sky anxiously. The lightning flashed more and more vividly, black clouds were coming nearer and nearer. What was a distant rumble soon became a near-by, long undertow of ominous sound. Nearer and nearer it came, until every flash was followed by a sound like ripping.

Mrs. Reece was very uneasy, for she did not like to have the children in the tents alone. But soon Betty and Hope came scampering through the dark to the cabin. They were surprised to see the older people up. Before long the boys also came to the cabin rubbing their eyes, yawning, and pretending not to care whether there was to be a cyclone or a cloud-burst.

For a while all sat waiting for the storm to break. When it did break, what torrents of rain and wind descended! How the trees groaned and cracked! How the rain roared upon the shingled roof, and how the wind howled through the mountain valley!

"Well," said Ben Gile, "let's have a fire in the fireplace, then we can have a crackle of our own." He had noticed how nervous Mrs. Reece grew, and that the little girls were watching her. He could not help thinking that it was foolish, even wicked, to waste strength in fear of something which no one of them could stop. "Build a fire, boys." And build a fire they did--a royal good blaze. "Now throw on some of those pine-cones you children gathered." There was a flare in the cabin almost as bright as the incessant flare of the lightning outside. "I'll tell you what we'll do," he continued, "we will have a midnight spread. We will have some of Tom's famous flapjacks. Mrs. Reece, don't you want to make molasses candy, and then the children can pull it."

The storm was forgotten by the children as, with many squeals of glee, they rushed into this midnight frolic.

"And now, Ben," said Tom, the guide, "I've just found something; I have it in my hand. I propose, Ben, while the rest of us work, that you make one of your stories out of it, and tell us all about it."

Tom opened his hand, and the children crowded around to see. There was a shout of laughter.

"Why, that's only a dead June-bug!"

"Who wants to know about a June-bug?" exclaimed Jimmie, much to the discomfiture of the guide, who knew a great deal about moose and deer and bears and beavers, even if he didn't know much about a June-bug. The guides had profound respect for the schoolmaster, Ben Gile, who was really too wise and kind to laugh at another's ignorance. But this is another story, and Jimmie learned better in the years to come.

"You're right, Tom," said Ben, "to want to know. Sometimes it's about these commonest things folks know the least. When I was a boy it was always so with me. There are several facts about a June-bug that are interesting. First, it is not a bug at all; and, second, it comes in May and not in June. It is really a May-beetle, and a great, clumsy, buzzing, blundering fellow it is, as careless about its appearance as it is about the way it enters a room. You know the old adage, 'Haste makes waste'? Perhaps it's the haste that makes the June-bug's untidiness. Beetles have hard wing covers--see these little shell-like casings?--to cover the more delicate wings underneath. The June-bug has wing covers, too, but it never keeps its best wings tucked in. They are always hanging out in a crumpled way. These bugs eat the leaves of the trees, and their children, little, fat, white grubs with horny heads, nibble, as they crawl around under the surface of the earth, the tender roots of the grass and the strawberry plants."

"Why, Ben, you've told me more already," said Tom, "than any dullard like me could ever learn from a book. To think it's a beetle! But I might have known from looking at it. Are all the beetles harmful?"

"Most of them are pests, and do a good deal of damage. Its cousin, rose-beetle, is pretty, her body covered with soft, yellow hairs, and she has rose-colored legs. But handsome is as handsome does, and rose-beetle causes more damage than her clumsy cousin, for Rose feeds on rose-bushes as well as on fruit trees. Indeed, almost everything that comes to her mill is grist. She's as bad--and worse--than the elm-beetle."

By this time the cooking molasses smelled so good, the cabin fire roared so pleasantly, and the smell of the flapjacks Adam was frying was so appetizing, that the children had quite forgotten the storm outside, and were having one of the jolliest frolics of their lives--one they never forgot.

"Tell us something more, sir," urged Jack, "about the beetles."

"There is one comical fellow who makes me think of Peter. In the books it is called a click-beetle, but it is also called a skip-jack because of the somersaults it can turn. On the under side of its thorax is a spine resting on the edge of a hole. This funny beetle, by pushing the spine down over the hole and then letting it go, throws itself up in the air with a sharp click."

"Oh, I know them," called Hope, "for I have seen them doing it, but I never knew how they did it!"

"And now," said Master All-Wise, very soberly, "after I tell you that the children of the click-beetle are called wire-worms, and that they eat and kill the roots of plants, I want to tell you about a beetle no one of you has ever seen--a most extraordinary beetle."

[Illustration: A. Lady-beetle. B. Burying-beetle. C. Oil-beetle.]

All were attention at once.

"Many years ago there lived away out in California a little, round, brownish, striped beetle, which crawled about and ate heartily of a plant called the sand-bur. One day one of the family happened to wander up to a nice, juicy potato plant. After eating its fill it probably looked up some of its brothers and sisters, and told them about these good plants growing in the fields. With one accord they left the sand-burs and began to eat the potato plant. Farther and farther they wandered, until thousands of them reached the eastern part of our country, eating the potato plants wherever they found them on the way. Now, these beetles are to be seen everywhere in our country, spoiling crop after crop."

By this time Jack's eager face was smiling, and he was looking questioningly at Ben Gile.

"What kind of a beetle do you suppose it was?" asked the old man.

Nobody knew. At last Jack ventured, "Was it a potato-bug, sir?"

"Yes."

"Oh, of course!" shouted the children. "Why didn't we think of that? But you said we had never seen it."

"So I did," said the guide, "and I don't believe there is one child here who has ever carefully watched the potato-bug. And there's the carpet-beetle, whose babies eat carpets unless your mother tempts them with pieces of red flannel. And there's the searcher-beetle, with its pretty green or violet wing covers, who is always on the search for caterpillars. And there's the fire-fly, which is a soft-bodied beetle.

"And there's the very useful little beetle we call the ladybug, which is not a bug, but a beetle. The ladybug is a great help to men who own fruit orchards in the West. All over the country are to be found little bugs called scale insects. These scales are very bad for trees, because with their long, slender beaks the scales pump out the sap. Sometimes they are so thick on the branch that they coat it entirely. You remember that I told you that one of these troublesome scales is the cottony-cushion scale, and that one day it was discovered that a lady-beetle from Australia liked these scales very much. So a great many of them were taken to California to eat the scales. The ladybugs eat little green aphids, too, and often Mrs. Ladybug will lay her eggs right in the midst of a family of aphids; and then the larv?are surrounded by a hearty lunch when they come out of the egg. They eat the aphids, the scales, and sometimes the eggs of other insects."

"Time, Ben," said Adam, "to have the flapjacks. I guess the storm must be blowing over."

All drew up to the cabin table, and ate as heartily as if they were eating dinner. It really looked as if the children had had no supper.

"In about half an hour," said Tom, "the storm will be over. Aren't there any beetles that live in the water, Ben?"

"Oh yes; you can see them any day if you go by a brook. The diving-beetles are skimming about, rowing themselves along with their flattened hind legs. Every few minutes they come to the surface and lift their wings to get a little air under them, then down they go into the brook. They are very hungry beetles, eating other insects which they find in the water. The boldest often try to take a bite out of a fish. Just think of calling a baby beetle a water-tiger! Well, these babies are as savage and ferocious to the little creatures living about them in the water as a big tiger would be to us, if we should happen to meet one.

"I like best the whirligig-beetles, they are such frisky fellows, always having a good time, frolicking about with dozens of other little whirligigs. They are bluish-black and shiny, and if you look carefully you will see a little bubble at the tip of every tail. This little bubble is held there by tiny hairs, and because whirligig has it, it can breathe while it stays under the water. From time to time it comes to the surface to get a new bubble, then is off again for another race or game of tag with its friends, and at the same time to snap up a few water creatures for dinner. It looks as though it had four eyes, but it has not, just two, divided into upper and lower halves. The upper halves look up through the water and the lower ones down at the bottom of the brooks. So, you see, insects must step lively if they want to keep out of its clutches.

"The babies of some beetles, instead of liking nice, clean food, prefer dead animals. The mother and father hunt around until they find a dead mouse or bird; then they begin to dig away the earth under the mouse or bird and around it. Finally the poor dead thing is in a deep hole; then Mrs. Burying-beetle lays her eggs on it, and together they cover it up with earth. When the grubs hatch they find plenty to eat, and are soon big burying-beetles, like their mothers and fathers.

"Did you ever wonder how the little fat worms get inside of chestnuts and acorns? A beetle called a weevil is the creature which puts the fat worms there. Mrs. Weevil has a long, slender, curved beak. She crawls up on to the side of a chestnut, bores a hole in the side, then lays an egg deep down in it. After a while the egg hatches and a tiny grub begins to feed on the nut. Fatter and fatter it gets; sometimes it lies in the nut all winter, but more often it crawls out and buries itself in the ground while it grows into a weevil.

"Some day, as you are walking along a sunny road in the country, you may meet a blister-beetle. It is a pretty, bluish-green color, and when you pick it up you will see drops of oil oozing out of its joints. The dried bodies will raise a blister on the skin, and that is the reason we call such beetles blister-beetles. There is a queer blister-beetle who lays her eggs near bees' nests. The baby beetles then wait for a bee to come along. They fasten themselves to the hairs on the bee's body. When the bee goes to its nest to put in the honey the young beetle manages to get into a honey-cell with the egg. Mrs. Bee does not see that anything is amiss, seals up the cell, and flies away for another load. The larva first eats the egg of Mrs. Bee, then it changes into a clumsy kind of a fellow, floats in the honey, and eats all it can so that it will quickly become a grown-up.

"There is one beetle which plants a tiny fungus in its home in the ground. The babies run along and eat the tips of this delicacy, while the mothers and fathers take larger bites. These are called ambrosia-beetles, because of the dainty food they eat. Now that the storm is over, I mustn't tell you anything more than a few words about the engraver-beetle, which lives between the bark and the live wood of a tree. Mr. and Mrs. Engraver-Beetle make a long tunnel under the bark. Mrs. Engraver makes notches along the sides, and in every notch lays an egg. When the babies hatch, each one begins a tunnel for itself, running out straight from the long one. And now that's the end of this story."

"Well, Ben," said Tom, respectfully, "these children don't know the value of the things they are learning. It's a privilege, sir, to have a chance to guide with you. I've learned more in these last years about God's wonders from you than ever I learned in all my long life. I didn't know there were so many beetles in the world."

"These are only half a dozen of a multitude of beetles which we haven't the time to name."

"Now, off to bed, children," said Mrs. Reece, "or you'll never be able to get up early. Good-night to every one!"

XIV

A DAY'S HUNTING

It was a glorious day after the night's storm. By five o'clock the children were ready to go hunting with Ben Gile.

Although they were rather sleepy, yet they managed to get an early breakfast--five o'clock is an early breakfast, isn't it?--and by six o'clock they were off into the woods. Ben Gile made the children follow behind him in single file, and so in line, making as little noise as possible, they went through the woods. The birch-trees and poplars, in the midst of the darker, heavier foliage, seemed golden with the early sunlight. Everywhere the bushes sparkled with the rain of the night before. They took a path that ran almost in a curve around one entire side of the mountain. Ben Gile kept a sharp lookout, for the partridge, he knew, would be upon the ground or up in the trees. He pointed to several places where partridge had been scratching. The woods were full of them, and every minute he expected to hear the whir of their wings as they started up. And, sure enough, there was suddenly a loud beating of wings, and then, crack! crack! crack! from the shot-gun. Down came three plump partridges. Not more than ten minutes later the old man brought down three more. Then he let Jack, who was a good shot, take his gun, and down came two more.

"Eight partridge," he exclaimed, "and quite enough for us all! We shoot only what we actually need for food, not a bird more. Oho! somebody else made a home here. Old Paw Bear has been tearing it out and licking his chops."

The children leaned forward, looking eagerly. "What was it?" they asked.

"Honey," said the guide. "Paw Bear has a sweet tooth for honey and berries."

"I should think the bees would sting him," said Jimmie.

"They do try to, but little he cares, with his thick coat of hair. Not a bit. The bees have another enemy, too, which is always hovering about to find a chance to get into the busy little house; that is the bee-moth. If she gets the least opportunity Mother Bee-Moth lays her eggs in the wax of the honeycomb, for the baby moths are very fond of wax. It's not an easy matter to get in when the bees are not looking, but she manages it quite often; and when the little larvas hatch out of the eggs, they eat the wax and the mischief is done. When Mother Bee-Moth is seen the bees rush upon her and sting her to death. They have good cause to hate her, for the wax is precious, hard to make and to mould into the little cells. It is not pleasant to have some miserable worm eat the roof from your head. Oftentimes the bees are so discouraged that they decide, as they talk it over in bee language, that it is easier to build a new home than to repair the old one. They settle upon an hour of departure, and off they go."

"But I didn't know," said Betty, "that bees live in their hives; I thought that they just stored their honey there."

"So did I," said Jimmie.

It was Jack's time to smile, for, a country boy, he had often watched the hives. "Couldn't you tell us something, sir? Here's a bit of the cone left."

"Do you want to hear?"

"Oh, I think bees are so interesting!" Betty clapped her hands.

[Illustration: LEAF-CUTTER BEE]

"Did you ever look closely at a bee? Their bodies are covered with hairs, unlike the hairs found on other insects, for each hair is a tiny plume. And their mouths, which they have to use for so many different things, are remarkably made; each part is formed to do a certain kind of work. First there are the strong biting jaws, then another pair of jaws joined to the lower lip, which move easily back and forth. This forms a sucking instrument, which the bees use for drinking nectar."

"My," exclaimed Peter, "it must be convenient to have two pairs of jaws!"

"On the head, too, are antenn? which form little elbows, like those of the ant. With these the bee smells and feels. Some bees have short tongues, and usually live alone; others have long tongues, and generally live in colonies. Perhaps a long tongue makes an insect sociable, and perhaps sociability makes a tongue grow long."

The children were looking at their tongues to see which had the longest. Peter scanned his anxiously. "Your tongue is awfully long, Pete," said Jack.

"I know an interesting short-tongued bee who lives in a house by herself. Her name is Andrena. She bores a hole in the ground, digging out a wide hallway. From this she digs side passages, each one ending in a little closed room. The walls of these rooms are hard and shiny, like porcelain. When Andrena finishes her house she makes a nourishing paste of nectar and pollen. Pollen is the yellow powder from flowers. You know bees, by carrying about the pollen, help in fertilizing the flowers. But of this we shall learn more some day when we are talking about the flowers. This powder the bee packs down into the little rooms. Then she lays an egg on each pile of food and builds a door to shut the egg away safely."

"Do bees always feed their children on nectar and pollen?" asked Hope.

"Always," replied the old man. "They never feed their babies on other insects, as the ants and wasps do. Then there are the little short-tongued bees who live in apartments, the apartments all clustered together, with a common wide passageway into the ground and separate hallways. Around the main opening is an odd chimney, built on a slant, which prevents the rain from pouring into the open doorway."

The children were wide-eyed with astonishment. That bees should build chimneys was more than they could believe!

"Goodness!" said Jimmie, "if that is what a short-tongued bee can do, what can a long-tongued bee do?"

"They are very clever. Some are carpenters, some masons, some miners, some tailors. The leaf-cutter bee makes a neat home, covering the walls with pretty, green leaves. First she digs a tunnel in a suitable branch of wood; then she goes to a rosebush, cuts out an oval piece of a rose leaf, and arranges it smoothly on the walls of the tunnel; cuts other oval pieces and puts them on, fastening the edges neatly together. In the bottom of the tunnel she puts some pollen paste, lays an egg on the paste, cuts some circular pieces of rose leaf, which she presses on the top of the egg and pollen, forming a green roof for the room and a floor for the room above. She puts in more food and another egg, until the tunnel is full of little rooms."

"And what does the carpenter-bee do?" asked Jack, looking with new respect at the bit of honeycomb he held in his hand.

"She makes doors of pith, and, like the tender mother she is, sits on top of the nest waiting for her babies to grow up. This is a most unusual thing for a bee mother to do. The egg at the very bottom of the tube hatches first, but it has to wait until the others hatch. By-and-by Mrs. Carpenter-Bee takes them all out for a sunny flight in the summer air."

"And they never come back any more!" sang out Peter.

"Indeed they do, you care-free youngster. The pith doors have been taken down, and they come back to put things in order. They clean house; they bring out every scrap piece by piece. There is a big carpenter-bee that makes its doors of chips of wood, usually neatly glued together. There is just one lazy bee in the world of which I know, and that is a visiting-bee."

"Visiting-bees?"

"Yes, the guest-bees, who visit their friends the year round, let their hosts wait upon them, and never help to keep anything clean or to collect nectar and pollen. Mrs. Guest-Bee even lays her eggs in Mrs. Bumblebee's nest, and when the guest babies hatch out, it is not their mother, but Mrs. Bumblebee, who feeds them from the food she has stored up for her own children. The guest-bees are so lazy that no little baskets are found on their legs for carrying pollen."

"But aren't the bees ever idle?" asked Peter, whose conscience hurt him because he never liked to work.

"No bee except the guest-bee and drone is ever idle. The happy-go-lucky bumblebee, which buzzes so near us on these warm summer days, is always on the go, although she is easy-going and happy-go-lucky. Mrs. Bumblebee isn't an over-particular person, as bee persons go. She is not a careful housekeeper, like her cousin Mrs. Honey-Bee, but she carries her own burdens just the same, and probably is as contented in her roughly made, untidy house as Mrs. Honey-Bee is in her beautifully neat one. Sometimes she has a nest as big as your head, with rooms in it of all sizes and shapes. She probably thinks the honey-bee family would get along just as well if they were a little less fussy, and probably she is right. Early in the spring Mrs. Bumblebee starts out house-hunting. When she finds the place she wants she puts some honey and pollen there, and lays an egg on the little pile. After a while the larvas come out of the eggs. When they have eaten what they want they make a cocoon, and curl up for a rest while they are being made into little workers. You know, the bee family is made up of the mother bee, who is called the queen, and many fathers, who are called drones; all the rest are workers."

"That's something like the ants, sir, isn't it?"

"Yes, something, Jack; but you mustn't tell that story yet. Every one of Mrs. Bumblebee's first family are workers. While the first workers are out getting food for their brothers and sisters, Mrs. Bumblebee takes the old cocoons which they have left behind and makes them over into rooms for the new babies, who are to be drones and queens.

"They are very happy all summer long, but as it grows colder they begin to shiver and shake. At last all die except the young queens, who have crawled away from the nest and found a warm crack somewhere in which to take a long nap. When the spring comes the young queens rub their eyes, stretch their legs and wings, and are off looking for a home for their coming families."

"But what kind of bee's-nest did old Paw Bear get into?" asked Hope.

"This nest was a wild honey-bee's nest. Some honey-bees are wild this way, but most live close to the homes of men. When they live in our gardens they live in a hive we make for them, and the families consist of Mrs. Honey-Bee, the queen, about a hundred Mr. Honey-Bees, and many thousands of workers. The workers are the little bees, the drones the middle-sized ones, and the queen is the great big bee.

"Men often help the workers to build the little cells in which they store the honey and in which the queen lays the eggs. These cells are six-sided rooms. Every day the queen lays an egg in one of the little rooms, and with it the workers put some pollen and honey. In three days out comes the larva from the egg. It is a helpless creature, soft and white, and without feet.

"Busy, busy workers are always on hand to take the best care of the babies. The first food the nurses give them is bee jelly, which looks something like blanc-mange. This bee jelly the workers make in their stomach, then feed it from their own mouths into the baby mouths. After lunching a couple of days on bee jelly they are old enough to eat pollen and honey, which the workers get out of the six-sided rooms where they have packed it away.

"These babies grow very quickly. Soon they are so long that they almost fill their rooms. Then the nurses put in some extra food, tuck in the babies, and make a roof of wax over each room. For a whole day the baby has to feed itself, shut away all alone; then it stops eating, and lies very quietly while it is being made into a real bee. In about thirteen days it splits its dried skin, in which it has been napping, gnaws a hole in the wax roof, and out it comes--a full-fledged bee.

"But it is too new and young to go out in the big world yet, so for a few weeks it is kept busy in the hive nursing other baby bees. When it has grown stronger it leaves the hive, flying out over the sunny pastures in search of buttercups and clover heads.

"Whenever the honey-bees want to make a queen they know just how to do it. You know, a queen is a very important person. A bee queen is like an ant queen, not the ruler of a kingdom, but the mother of many, many children. Since a queen is a person of such note, she must have a larger room than an ordinary worker, so they set to work and tear down the partitions between two or three cells. When the egg in the large room hatches the white larva is fed bee jelly, just like the little worker larva, but it is never given any pollen or honey. When it is five days old some jelly is put in the room with it and a roof is built over its head. For seven long days the baby stays here all alone, then it gnaws its way out, and, wonder of wonders, we have a queen instead of a worker!

"Now, Mrs. Honey-Bee has been the queen of the family so long she is very angry to have a young queen hatch out, and does all she can to kill her. But the workers have spent much time and labor in making this queen, and they stand close around her to protect her from the jealous old queen. The honey-bee family, however, has grown so big that there is room for no new babies in the hive, and that is the reason that the workers have raised a new queen, so that she may start a new family.

"There is not room in one house for two queens; one must go, and It is usually old Mrs. Honey-Bee. Surrounded by part of the family, she flies out of the old home in search of a new place. If she is living in some one's garden a new hive is all ready for her, and she soon settles down again to her egg-laying, while the workers hurry to bring in food for the new babies. If there is no hive ready for this exiled family, it swarms in a tree or any other good place it happens to find."

"Yes," said Betty; "but do the workers have to work all the time?"

"They do everything except the egg-laying. All the pollen and honey must be brought into the hive by them. Have you ever seen the little baskets which working bees have for carrying pollen? Perhaps you do not know what pollen is. Well, some day look right down in the centre of a flower and you will find some fine yellow powder. That is pollen, or bee bread, and the bees are very fond of it. On the hind leg of the worker is a nice smooth place, and on each side of it are stiff, curved hairs which cover it over. Into this little cage the bees push the pollen, then fly swiftly away toward the hive. Here this heavily laden little fellow stands over one of the rooms and pushes the pollen off his hind legs by scraping with his middle legs.

"You have eaten honey, and know how thick and sweet it is. Very unlike the sweetened water in the flower-cups, isn't it? The bees make this honey out of the watery nectar, and I will tell you how they do it. The bee sips this sweet nectar into its mouth, then the nectar goes down a tiny tube into a little pouch called the honey sac. This sac opens into the stomach, but between the two are little lips which guard the entrance. If the worker is hungry the little lips open, and the nectar goes from the honey sac into the stomach. But if it wants to carry it back to the hive the lips stay tightly closed. When the honey sac is full the worker flies back to the hive and empties it into one of the rooms.

"Then a number of bees stand with their heads bent downward and move their wings just as fast as they can, looking like miniature electric fans. Of course they grow very warm, and this makes the hive warm. This warm air evaporates the extra water in the nectar, and soon the honey is all finished. These bees which beat the air so tirelessly keep the hive fresh and sweet, which is very necessary when so many bees live in one house.

"The workers make the cells as well as fill them, and now a very queer thing happens. A great many bees eat a great deal of honey. They eat all they can hold, then crawl up to the top of the hive. There are as many there as can find room; the rest hang on to these until a curtain of bees is formed. Sometimes they hang quietly and patiently for several days until, on the under side of the abdomen, tiny shining plates of wax appear. Other workers break off these pieces of wax and build them up into cells. You know how big a pound is, don't you? Well, just think how many, many times the bees must carry honey to the hives when I tell you that twenty-one pounds of honey will make but one pound of wax. Bees are very economical with their wax. When they have to patch up holes and fill in cracks in their hives they do it with a gum which they scrape off sticky buds.

"All summer long these workers are laying in food to keep this large family during the cold weather. If for any reason the supply of food is low the workers sting the babies to death rather than have them starve. Is it any wonder that these workers, who have so much to do and so many cares from morning until night, die very young? The queen may live for two or three years, but the workers do not live longer than six or eight weeks."

"Goodness me!" said Jimmie, "I wouldn't have believed there was any insect on the face of the earth as clever as those bees! If insects were all like that, I'd want to know about every one of them. Can't you tell us something of the wasp? They must be clever fellows, too."

"Not to-day," answered Ben Gile; "it is getting toward noon, and we must start home for dinner and to get our partridge cooked. Pick up the birds, Jack, and put them in your game-bag. We must be off."

XV

LEAVING CAMP

At last the day had come, and the children were to leave Camp-in-the-Clouds. They had been there for one whole glorious week of fishing, hunting, camping, picnicing, stories, and sleeping in tents. Betty and Jimmie felt rather sober, for the time for them to go back to the city was drawing near. A week now, and their good times for the summer would be over. Already the leaves were turning a little, and the air growing crisper every day. Indeed, up in Camp-in-the-Clouds they had twice in the early morning to break the ice on the spring in order to get the water, and at night the blankets felt warm and cosey. Betty and Jimmie liked their city home, and after they were once in it they enjoyed their school work, too. They had many friends, entertainments, parties, and made many expeditions to the Zoo and to the parks. But, somehow, the happiest days of all the year came in the summer in Rangeley Village. Every hour seemed precious to them now, and the fingers on Betty's right hand--the number of days that were left--were all too few. Even Jimmie, who cared less for the country than Betty did, was sorry. And the children were sorry to have them go. All through the cold, white winter in Rangeley Village they were expecting the Reece children and the old guide. With their coming, good times began again.

And this morning, on which they were leaving camp, they felt rather blue, for, although they expected to come back the next summer, as indeed they did, yet it seemed such a long, long time to wait! They followed Ben Gile single file down the mountain at a good pace, but without saying very much. By noon they had reached the Dead River Ponds, and were ready for luncheon.

"I think some of that birch, Tom," said Ben Gile, "would make a good fire for us."

[Illustration: A. Feeding the baby wasps. B. A grown-up wasp.]

Tom, who was a famous woodchopper in winter, went off toward the tree, followed by lazy little Peter, who loved to see others work. Soon the chips were flying right and left. Suddenly there was a yell from Peter. Tom dropped his axe. Ben Gile hurried over to the boy, and the others crowded around. Tom was sure a splinter had gone into Peter's eye. The lad was holding on to his eye, and jumping up and down with pain. But as Ben Gile was trying to make the boy take his hand away, Tom exclaimed, grabbed one hand with the other, and made for the pond. "It's hornets, Ben!" he called; and before the others could say anything he had clapped some mud on his own hand and brought mud for Peter's eye, which he poulticed with this useful material, and tied around it a big white handkerchief. Although Peter did not in the least like the bite, yet he felt rather proud of the bandage, and for the first time in his life he, too, wanted to know about the creatures who could give so much pain.

"Tell us, sir," the children cried, "about the wasps while dinner is cooking."

So Ben Gile, who had left the cooking to the other guides, gathered the children and Mrs. Reece about him, and began: "One day last fall I saw, high up in a tree near the pond, the pretty, gray nest of Mrs. Vespa-Wasp. It did not look like a real house, with windows in it and steps leading up to it. But there it hung, swinging in the bare branches, its walls of pretty, soft gray blending so beautifully with the pale-blue sky.

"I wondered whether any of the wasp family was at home, but the house was too high for me to reach, so I went away to find a long pole with which to knock. With my long pole I knocked gently at first, then louder and louder, but no one stirred within. So I poked harder, trying to break off a strong branch which ran straight through the top of the house. At last it broke off, and down came the gray house almost into my arms.

"It was big and round, like a Japanese lantern. Guess of what it was made? Just paper. But not our kind of paper; it was wasp-paper. Mrs. Vespa and her family make this paper out of wood-pulp, which they get by scraping off the weathered wood from trees and fences. Of course this old wood is of various colors, but that makes the house so much the prettier. One wasp comes back with its burden of woody pulp rolled up in a little pellet. This it takes and spreads in thin ribbons along the edge of the wall which is being made. Perhaps this edge is dark gray. Then off it flies for more material, while another takes its place with a pellet of light gray, which is soon skilfully moulded on to the edge. Sometimes the outer wall consists of several layers of this wasp-paper, which is strong and waterproof. Within the wall are many stories of cone, built like different floors in our own houses.

"Early in the spring Mrs. Vespa-Wasp, who has been passing the cold winter days tucked away in a warm crevice somewhere, comes out and finds a site for her summer home. She begins this as a very small and simple one, starting with just a few rooms fastened to the branch of a tree. Here she lays an egg in each little room, then brings in food for the new baby wasps which are in the making. The kind of food which is stored away depends upon the kind of wasps. Some like beetles, some spiders, some caterpillars, and others grasshoppers and cicadas.

"As in the bee family, the first children are all workers, because Mrs. Vespa-Wasp needs assistance in building up the home and feeding the children. This first home is small, not nearly large enough for the growing family, so new rooms must be built at once. These are added on to the first ones until there is a good-sized layer of them. If Mrs. Wasp should go on making this upper story larger and larger, it would be buffeted about by the wind and rain, and perhaps broken. So the family starts a second story under the first. On the under side of the top floor some of the cells are broken away and a stem is made to start the next floor, and so on, until there are four or five combs in the house. They are always building the house over, tearing down the walls to make room for new floors; but this does not make the house unsafe in the mean time, as the walls are not connected with the floors, but form a loose envelope about them.

"Later in the season, after the family has become very large, some of the upper cells are torn out, making a nice, warm attic, where the family may go to keep out of the wind and rain. They dislike the cold and wet very much.

"I carried this big house to my cabin with me, so that I might look it over and see just how it was arranged. Very carefully I cut away a little of the outer wall until I had a place large enough to look through. Guess what I saw lying cuddled down in many of these rooms? Little, soft, white baby wasps. When the Vespa family are grown up they are called hornets, and Peter and Tom know how hornets sting! I was not afraid of the babies, but was not sure that all the old wasps were out. It was a cold day, and wasps get stiff very quickly, so I watched carefully to see whether the warm air of the room would not limber up some stiff joints which were perhaps in hiding up-stairs in the house. Sure enough, in a few moments out crawled a worker, looking quite dazed and sheepish at the change in temperature. I did not wait for it to become thoroughly awake, but picked it up with the forceps and put it out of the window. I was kept busy, for twenty-five old fellows walked out, thinking, no doubt, that they had made a mistake in the season, and that it was not time, after all, for them to die. All the wasp family, except the queens, expect to die, and do die in the autumn.

"I could not find either flies or spiders for the babies, and even if there had been a few about I could not have used them, as there was no worker wasp to chew them soft and fine for them. So I made a nice, appetizing syrup of sugar and water, and found that young wasps were as eager for sweets as little children are. They worked their baby mouths busily as long as I had the patience to feed them. When the Vespa family are grown up they eat honey dew from the little aphids, fruit juice, and the nectar from flowers, or, if fortune favors them, they may gain entrance to Mrs. Honey-Bee's home, and feast from her well-filled honeycombs. But the babies all eat insects which their mothers put in the little rooms beside the eggs.

"Mrs. Polistes is a cousin of Mrs. Vespa. She is long and slender, while Mrs. Vespa is rather broad. Her house is a much simpler affair. It has just one layer of rooms suspended by a stem from the under side of a porch, or maybe the eaves, of a house."

"Are there solitary wasps," asked Jimmie, "just as there are solitary bees?"

"Many wasps prefer to live alone rather than in a big house with hundreds of others. They are like bees in their cleverness, knowing how to tunnel in wood, dig deep pits in the ground, or make nests of mud. Mr. Kellogg, a very wise man, and young to be so wise, tells of one interesting little wasp, called the thread-waisted sand-digger, which lives in California in the salt-marshes. These marshes are covered by plants, but in between are little smooth places covered with a glistening crust of salt. It is in these open spots that Mrs. Sand-Digger makes her home. She has strong jaws, and with these she cuts out a neat little circle of salty crust. Then she begins to dig a tunnel, humming away to herself all the time. After the hole is ready she very carefully backs out of it and puts a circular door on.

"Then she flies away to find food to store up for her children. These babies like tender, green inch-worms, so Mrs. Digger-Wasp hunts around until she finds a fat one, and then proceeds to paralyze it, so that it will stay quietly in the house until the babies are ready to eat it, for baby digger-wasps are little cannibals, preferring living caterpillars to any pre-digested spiders or flies. It is very wonderful that Mrs. Digger-Wasp knows where to sting a caterpillar in order to paralyze it and yet not kill it. But she does. Perhaps you remember that insects have knots of nerve cells, connected by nerve threads, extending from one end of the body to the other? Jimmie remembers that I pinched him to illustrate this point. The knot on the top of the food-tubes is the brain, then underneath there are usually three in the thorax and several in the abdomen. Well, Mrs. Digger-Wasp stings one or more of these little knots, which we call ganglia. That paralyzes the young inch-worm, so that it becomes limp and helpless, but still lives. Then Mrs. Wasp picks it up and carries it to her house, and packs it in the bottom of the tunnel.

"After putting in five or ten she lays an egg, fastening it on the body of one of the worms. She backs out of the tunnel, and flies off to collect balls of dirt. With these she fills up the tunnel completely. Carefully she puts the little round door on. One day some one saw her do a curious thing. She wished to be very sure that the door was fast shut. Perhaps it did not fit well. So she found a tiny pebble, held it in her jaws, and hammered the door down with it. Wasn't that a clever thing for a wasp to do? The door closed, this is all the attention she gives to baby digger-wasps. She has put in plenty of food, even for the hungriest larva. Now it must look out for itself, eat, grow fat and strong, and then dig its way out into the salt-marsh.

"Mrs. Eumenes is a good-looking little wasp dressed in black and yellow. She is a mason, making a pretty mud vase for a home. The clay, or mud, she moistens, then moulds it, little by little, into the vase, which she fastens on to a twig. Some mud-daubers make small cylinders placed side by side. Into these they put stung spiders, after tearing off their legs to make sure they will not recover and run away before the eggs hatch. Sometimes the mud-daubers plaster up the keyholes in a house, and so have snug homes.

"One day last summer, as I was sitting outside my cabin, I noticed a wasp carrying something green in its mouth. It came close to my head, then finally crawled up under the shingles on the side wall. All the afternoon it came and went, each time bringing something green. The next afternoon I was loading my guns, and had put a hollow gun-barrel on a table at my side. Soon I heard a whir of insect wings, and there, on the table, was my wasp friend. It walked up and down, examining very carefully the hollow barrel, then cautiously it crawled in. In about five minutes it crawled out again and flew away. Soon it was back with a piece of green in its mouth. It crawled into the barrel and left the green. Six times the wasp did this; then my curiosity became so great I could wait no longer. When she flew away I tapped the barrel on the table and emptied out six little green worms, all limp and still. But Mrs. Wasp was back again, and I guiltily withdrew. She had brought the seventh worm, and when she saw the six lying on the table she was much puzzled. She went around and poked each one to see whether it was limp, fearing, perhaps, that she had not stung them hard enough; but, finding them helpless, she picked them up one by one and patiently carried them back into the gun-barrel. Three times I emptied them out, and three times she put them back, then flew away, never to return. I suppose the last time she went in she laid the egg among the little worms, and then, her duty done, was off to find another good place to start a family.

"Have you ever seen a big cicada which makes the long, rasping sound in the trees? Some wasps like these very much for food. So, when cicada sings, Mrs. Wasp swoops down on it, stings it, and then, big and clumsy as it is, carries it to her home for her children to feast upon."

"A cicada is three or four times as large as a wasp, isn't it?" asked Mrs. Reece.

"Yes; but there is nothing the wasps can't do," replied Ben Gile.

"I should think not!" exclaimed Peter, who by this time was able to smile again.

"The trout are ready, Ben," said Adam, "and everything else, too, I guess."

With running and laughter the children were soon about the fire, eating their last delicious out-of-door dinner.

XVI

EYES AND NO EYES

The evening party at Ben Gile's cabin was to be the last of all the beautiful summer, for the next day Betty and Jimmie were to leave with their mother for the city, and this was the evening which was to decide who was to receive the prize.

Betty had been working very hard for it, and wanted it. But Jimmie couldn't see any use in lying with your nose on an ant-hill. As for Peter, he giggled whenever ants were mentioned to him, and seemed not to care much one way or another. Hope, however, was often with Betty, and the two girls, flat on the grass, tried to discover as many mysteries as they could about the busy little fellows. As for Jack, he was as busy as the ants, following them about, lying quietly for hours, and borrowing any book he could find that would tell about them. It seemed to him that if he could have that magnifying-glass, that book of colored plates, and the five-dollar gold piece, he would be the richest boy in all the world! He thought about it by night and by day, and he was certain that with the insect book and the glass, he should discover things nobody else in the world had ever seen.

The poor boy was trembling with eagerness on this evening of the party at the guide's cabin. The children took their turn in telling what they knew. Peter giggled, and said they seemed to lug a good deal of food. Jimmie said they ran in and out of their ant hills very fast, and knew how to build big hills. Hope was so frightened that, when it came her turn, the child could not tell even the little she knew.

But Betty, who loved everything in the out-of-door world, forgot herself and her fright in the true love which she had for natural history. She said she had spent hours in a neighborhood of ants, near the doorways they had in the ground. Some of the doorways were large, and some were small, and the little ants who went in and out of the doors carried off the pieces of cake she fed to them. Sometimes the crumbs were three or four times as big as the ants. She had seen two little ants attack a large piece of cake, but it proved too much for them, so one mounted guard over it while the other scurried off. In a few moments it came back with a whole squad of ants, who surrounded the cake and pushed and pulled with all their might. They actually got it to the door, Betty said, and after that she could see it no more. Then Betty spoke a little wistfully: "If only I had been an ant I could have gone down after it. I could have seen what they did with it, sir."

"Well, my dear," said Ben Gile, "if you want to see what they do, start a colony of them some day in a glass case. That will solve a good many of your problems. And now, what else?"

"I saw them doing a good deal that was interesting, sir, but I couldn't understand it."

"It's your turn, Jack. We will come back to Betty by-and-by."

"I found out, sir, that in every ant colony there are always three kinds of ants--the queens, the males, and the workers. It's much like what you told us of the bees. And it seemed to me, sir, every time I looked at them, that they were happy together, busy with their work and never quarrelling with one another. I suppose they were happy because each one had some special work to do. I looked it all up in the books, and I found that some are born queens, to be waited on, while others are born workers, to do the serving. But they are all contented.

"The queen ant is not a real queen ruling a little kingdom; she is the mother ant, and lays all the eggs. She is well cared for and protected by the workers. These are the active little ants who do the work. They are happy, too, running about, digging new passageways, clearing the paths to their front doors, and bringing in food, which they store in their granaries. Some ants, sir, build their tunnels very deep underground. A doorway opens into a wide gallery, from which others branch and wind their way down into the dark ground. Sometimes they build a high mound around the entrance, and often a large colony will have many such mounds."

[Illustration: A. Honey ant. B. Ants exchanging greetings.]

"Some ants," added Ben Gile, "dig out their homes in dead logs or hollow stems. I know of one little fellow who is clever enough to build a shed. It hunts around to find decayed wood. This it chews into a fine pulp, then spreads it out into a roof; sometimes it is a good-sized roof. This same ant dearly loves the honeydew which aphids secrete. So in order to protect these helpless little green bugs, and make them as comfortable and contented as possible, they build a neat shed over them. When the ants wish a dainty luncheon of honeydew they crawl up under the little shed and get a drink of this sweet juice. Although a colony of ants lives together so peacefully, Jack, they are apt to be very quarrelsome with their neighbors; often they go to war with another colony if the members of that colony happen to trespass on their grounds."

"I found out about some naughty, lazy ants, sir. Instead of taking care of their own homes and hunting up their own food, they go out to war against another kind of ant, which is living quietly and attending to its own business. All the grown-up ants these little fighters either kill or frighten so that they run away as fast and as far as their legs will carry them. Then these lazy ants steal the eggs and the babies. Some of them they eat on the way home, but most of them they carry to their underground galleries. There they take good care of them until they are grown up. Then these stolen babies become the slaves of the lazy ants; but the poor little slaves have never known any other life, so they cheerfully serve their masters, doing everything for them; in fact, so long have these masters had little slaves to wait upon them that they do not know at all how to look out for themselves. They have been known to starve to death rather than to feed themselves."

"But there are many respectable ants," objected Ben Gile, "and I will tell you how a well-regulated household behaves. One day last summer, when I was walking in the afternoon, I found myself suddenly surrounded by a cloud of winged insects--thousands and thousands of them. I caught one of them and found that it was a winged ant, for the males and queens have wings with which to fly away on their wedding journey. This journey lasts only a short time, and usually many colonies fly up together in the bright summer air. The wedding journey is a picnic for hungry birds. Just think of finding such a mass of juicy morsels at one time. They fly into the crowd and eat as many of the ants as they can. But many escape. At last they become exhausted. The males fall to the ground and die. The queens break off their wings, because they never need them after the wedding journey.

"They look about for a good place to start a new home. The first thing the queen does is to lay her eggs in a neat little pile. These soon hatch out into larv? tiny, worm-like grubs without any legs. Queen ants feed their babies faithfully with nice, tender insects, which they chew for them. Sometimes these larv?spin a tiny cocoon, in which they lie quietly while they are being made over into ants--perhaps into a queen, like the mother, or a male, like the father; perhaps into a worker, which is the mainstay of the whole colony. This first family of babies the queen mother must look out for herself, but just as soon as the baby workers are grown up it is their turn to help her.

"The first set of workers are very small. From morning until night they are busy. Early in the morning they must go out for food, to catch insects for the queen's breakfast and for the queen's baby ants. To be sure, it does not take long to prepare this meal, as it is chewed for the babies instead of cooked. Then the house must be set to rights, extra grains of sand must be cleared out of the paths and galleries. Perhaps some careless little girl or boy may have stepped on the mound around the entrance and crushed it. The workers hurry to clear away the ruins, and soon have a new mound neatly piled up. Tell us, Jack, what you know about these workers."

Jack's face was bright with eagerness. "Well, sir, in ant homes there are always babies, lots of them, just as in other homes. These little larv?must be fed often and kept clean. The workers are the nurses as well as housekeepers. If the babies happen to be in a cool, damp part of the house they must be carried into a warmer, drier place. So the workers pick them up and take them out for an airing. Often they carry the little cocoons out into the warm sunshine or move them about from place to place. In some families of ants there are some with very big heads and strong jaws. These are the soldiers. If there is any trouble in their village these big-headed fellows go out as scouts or act as sentinels around the ant-hill. But the head of the worker is rather small. It's a clever head, though, sir. On it are two antenn? bent, sir, like sharp little elbows. You told us that ants talk with their antenn? These feelers are very sensitive. I watched two ants one day and saw them rubbing them together."

"I am sure," said Ben Gile, "that some very exciting and interesting conversations are carried on by these fellows."

"Back of the head," continued Jack, "is the thorax, with the six legs, then a very narrow piece joining the thorax and abdomen."

"I know of one ant," added the guide, "who is nothing more or less than a honey-jar. This honey-ant hangs by its legs from the roof of its home. The little workers go out and visit the oak-trees and hunt around for balls called oak galls. From these they get honey, which they carry home and feed to the little fellows hanging on the ceiling by their heels. The honey is stored away in their crops. All day these honey-jar ants are fed, until the abdomens are as big as a currant, and the sweet, yellow honey shines through the skin. When any of the family gets hungry it crawls up to one of these fat little fellows and takes a refreshing sip."

"I know of another ant," began Jack, who could scarcely wait to begin, "who lives in the home of a larger ant. This one builds small tunnels connected with the large ones of the big ant, but is careful to make the doorways so small that the big ones cannot creep in and eat up the babies. When Little Ant gets hungry it crawls up on Big Ant's back. Very gently it strokes its head, then licks its cheek until the mouth of Big Ant fairly waters. This is just what Little Ant intends the mouth shall do. It laps up the drop of sweetness, crawls down, climbs on the back of another big ant, and has a second luncheon. Sometimes little thief ants live in other ants' houses, stealing the food which the workers have been so busy collecting all the long day."

By this time the children were listening in open-eyed astonishment to Jack, who had absorbed so much of the spirit and the information of the old guide that he could talk almost as interestingly.

"Mother aphids," interrupted Ben Gile, "who like corn very well, lay their eggs at the roots of the corn. But if the babies hatch out before the corn roots are ready there is a family of ants who come to the rescue. They carry these babies over to some other roots, where they may feed until the corn roots grow. Later they carry them carefully back again. Of course, they do not do this because they care for the welfare of the aphids, but because they know if the little corn lice have plenty to eat they themselves will have plenty of honeydew, which they love."

"And there's a harvester, sir, who builds a big mound around its front door and carefully clears away the grass. Into the long galleries of its home it carries a great many seeds, and stores them away. All the chaff and hard parts which it cannot eat it carries out again."

"Leading up to the big mound," added Ben Gile, "are clear pathways as distinct as any path you or I make through the grassy fields. Perhaps ants are too little to do very much thinking, but they do many things which you and I would have to think about a long time before we should be able to do them.

They have a good government which runs along without friction. They can build roads, dig tunnels, spin silken webs, build sheds, go to war, harvest grain into the storehouses, and keep a farm of aphids."

By the time the old guide had finished Betty was waving her hand the way she did in school. "Please, sir, I don't know half as much as Jack does. He has told all I know, and more, too."

Ben Gile smiled at Betty, for he was very fond of her. He stroked his white beard, and went on smiling as if he had some pleasant thought in the back of his head. "Well, now, we must decide who has won the prize. Mrs. Reece, what do you think?"

Mrs. Reece was proud of her Betty, and would rather have had her the generous little girl she was than have her win all the prizes in the world. "I think Jack has abundantly earned the prize."

"And now, children, what do you think?"

"Jack!" they all shouted.

"Jack," said the guide, bringing forward three parcels, "here is the five-dollar gold piece--this will help you buy what you need; here is the book, which will help you to identify what you see; and here is the magnifying-glass. Remember, my boy, as you look through it, that it is God's work you are seeing. We have been through the old story of 'Eyes and No Eyes' with you boys. Peter, I'm afraid, goes out and sees nothing. You, Jack, have used your eyes, and already you have learned much that ought to make you a wiser man. As you look through the glass it is well to reflect that you will never see a cathedral window as beautiful as some wings you look upon, from the clear lights of the cicada's wing to the gorgeous dyes of the moth. You will never see groin or arch or hinge more wonderful than the covers of a wing or the exquisite joint of some little insect. You may travel the world over before you can find, made by man's hand, such mystery and beauty as lie about you in the natural world. All the dynasties of Egypt could not shape the scale on a moth's wing. All the religion of the past can shape nothing that will do the Creator so much reverence as the world He has created, the world we have about us. There, my boy, that is a long sermon, but you will profit by it, for the world will hear of you yet.

"And now there's a little girl in this room who has worked faithfully to find out what she could. She is five years younger than you, Jack, and I want her to have something, too."

For a minute Jack looked troubled; then he said, resolutely, "Let me give her my book, sir."

"No, no, Jack," replied Ben Gile, pleased with the lad's generosity. "I have an extra book here." Betty's face was beaming. "Now let me write in your books; then to supper, around our last camp-fire for this summer."

In a few minutes the children were about the fire, and there was the smell of roasting corn, the sizzle of broiling partridge tied around with bacon, and the fragrance of coffee for the older people. The firelight seemed particularly jolly. Betty was very happy with her book (nor would she be parted from it the next day on the train), and Jack was radiant. They ate and talked and sang about the camp-fire, thought Ben Gile the wisest man in the world, Mrs. Reece the kindest of mothers, hoped that next year would come soon, and wanted to know what stories they were to hear when the long winter was over.

"Perhaps it will be birds," said the guide; "perhaps fish; perhaps flowers; maybe it will be spiders and crabs. Next summer is a long way off. And now I have to go back to my school."

In a short time a line of lanterns was seen swinging and dancing up the hill of Rangeley as the children filed homeward. The summer was over.

www.ingramcontent.com/pod-product-compliance
Lightning Source LLC
Chambersburg PA
CBHW062015280526
45787CB00005B/2104